THE LAND CHANGED ITS FACE

The Evacuation of Devon's South Hams 1943-1944

THE LAND CHANGED ITS FACE

The Evacuation of Devon's South Hams 1943-1944

Grace Bradbeer

David & Charles : Newton Abbot

0 7153 5781 6

Set in 10-point Pilgrim 3-point leaded
and printed in Great Britain
by W J Holman Limited Dawlish
for David & Charles (Holdings) Limited
South Devon House Newton Abbot Devon

DEDICATION

To those who have helped me in so many different ways to write this piece of Devon history I give my grateful thanks

Contents

List of Illustrations

PLATES *Page*

IN TEXT

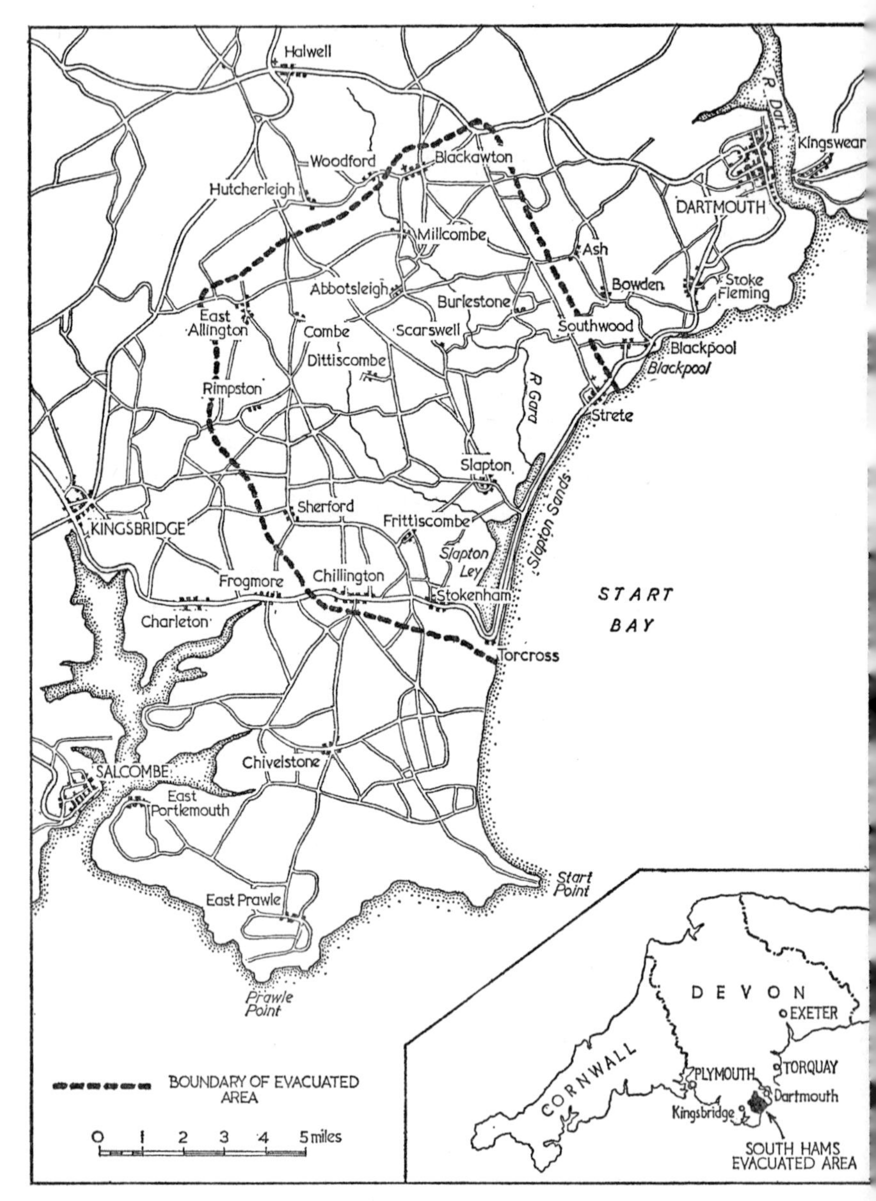

Map of the South Hams

Preface

THIS IS NOT A HISTORY BOOK IN THE STRICT SENSE OF the word, but an account of what took place in a little part of the English countryside in the last six weeks of 1943 and the first six months of 1944, during World War II. One of the most fertile pieces of agricultural land in the country was then sacrificed, so that Britain's American allies could receive a special training in preparation for the invasion of Normandy on D Day, 6 June 1944.

During that time I was a twice-weekly driver for the Women's Voluntary Service (now the Women's Royal Voluntary Service)—a humble enough contribution to the war effort, but one day, in spite of petrol rationing which allowed only the most essential journeys, I was asked to report to an Information Centre in the village of Blackawton in the South Hams, over twenty miles away from my normal base. It was the end of November 1943 and time was getting short I was told. When I reached Blackawton on that very dark, wet November morning I was asked immediately to fetch a farmer from an outlying farm, take him to Kingsbridge to see his solicitor, and then take him home again. Reporting back at the Centre, I was given another such errand,

and so on until the end of the day.

What impressed me most was the almost complete silence in the hitherto busy little villages which now seemed almost wholly deserted. A rat sauntered nonchalantly across a street, as if confident that no human would chase him, there were no animals to be seen in farmyards or fields, but a curious strip of matting lay on one field—'put there as a landing for planes', one of my passengers told me, for he was as interested in it as I was.

In the stringent secrecy of war time, however, one's interest and speculation went largely unsatisfied. All I had been told at a briefing was that 3,000 people in this rural area, their pets, their household possessions, their farm stock and equipment, were being completely moved elsewhere to help the war effort. Only six weeks had been allowed for the whole operation, and I learned while there that Americans were coming to practice warfare, though scarcely anyone spoke of the troops who were coming as they were all too concerned with the immediate and difficult problems. Outside the Area few knew that anything at all was going on. Only later was it made clear to people elsewhere exactly why the inhabitants had been obliged to pack up and leave.

Some years after the war, it occurred to me that this Evacuation of part of the South Hams was a piece of history which, brief though its span was, should be recorded before it was forgotten entirely. So, on many occasions, spread over a period of about two years, I visited that rural district to talk to the people whose lives had been so utterly disrupted. Subsequently I decided to put this information together into a book where it would appear in a more detailed and permanent form.

The surprising lack of any records adds to the need for the story to be told. For instance, every transaction taking place in the two Information Centres was noted daily at the time, but regrettably all were destroyed at the end of the war. Kingsbridge

Rural District Council, which controlled the Area, has nothing much to offer and, surprisingly, neither has the Devon County Council, though they do have the minutes of the County Emergency Committee referring to the Evacuation. It is not possible even to find an official map, though the Area can be traced easily by marking out the six parishes concerned on the ordnance survey map of Devon. The *Kingsbridge Gazette* made a few cautious references to the exercises at the time but obviously they could not say much. Perhaps one should have a certain sympathy with a member of the Kingsbridge Council who said, 'We just can't keep everything.'

Nevertheless, the story of the Exodus and Occupation, although only one of the many different episodes taking place in the British Isles during those war years, represents, in its way, a unique kind of personal sacrifice. Had it not taken place, the troops who landed in France on D Day 1944 would not have been so well prepared, and the course of the war for the Allies might have taken a very different turn. So it is because of the interest that delving into the past has given me that I have great pleasure in offering this tiny but important piece of history of the South Hams in 1943-44.

G.L.B.

Bovey Tracey

ONE
Peace and Plenty

THE SOUTH HAMS DISTRICT, CONSISTING OF THOSE essentially rural South Devon parishes which lie to the west and south of the River Dart, is not really like any other part of Devon. Although there is much beauty to be found over the whole county, the different neighbourhoods vary considerably, each one having its own particular charm. The South Hams has charm indeed. It has always been fertile and well farmed and the famous herds of South Devon cattle, the bountiful crops and interesting wild life, so beloved by ornithologists and botanists, have all combined to give it a special quality; and as if to reinforce its beauty the sea encircles the southern border like a frill of lace. There are a number of beautiful sandy beaches and also, stretching southwards in a gentle arc from Strete Gate to Torcross, there is the coarse shingle beach of Slapton Sands on which the events of this book so largely depend.

Much of the land is a rolling plateau of up to 600 feet above sea level, so that steep grass-covered cliffs rise from the coastline for a greater part of the district, while deep coombs run down to the sea and many little lanes, relics of packhorse days, criss-cross each other. Not until after World War I were many of these lanes given hard surfaces; they were mostly grassy tracks with high banks topped with thick hedges which combined to give shelter and protection to grazing stock from sudden rain and squalls and the sleet and cold winds of winter. The high banks still create shelter for quantities of wild flowers, great patches of violets, primroses, forget-me-nots, buttercups—all the old familiar treasures as well as unusual and rare species which are now duly noted and catalogued by enthusiasts. And everywhere there is, even today, a feeling of quiet contentment and peace.

The district is, geographically speaking, a relatively isolated one. Most of it thrusts out southwards from the gradual south-west inclination of the English coastline so that first the mail coach, and then the railway route joining Exeter and Plymouth, ran only along its northern fringe. Apart from a railway branch line to Kingsbridge (now closed) and a number of lesser-scale roads, the area between the main routes and the coast at Bolt Head, Prawle Point and Start Point was for centuries well and truly 'off the map'. Dartmouth, an important port in Norman times—for a long time more important than Plymouth—never had a railway station. The traveller had to go to Kingswear on the opposite of the Dart and complete the journey by ferry, for the first bridge crossing was some miles up-river at Totnes. This is still true today.

Life in the South Hams went on more or less undisturbed for centuries. True, there were sporadic skirmishes on the beaches, especially in medieval times, but generally only the local fishermen dragged their boats up and down the shingle ridges. Of course when smuggling became a profitable business there were clandestine beachings in the darkness, a subject not usually discussed very freely, though one well-to-do woman openly stated that her family's fortunes were founded, generations back, on smuggling. Even right into the twentieth century, life went on relatively unchanged in the busy hamlets and villages where the old cob cottages were huddled together in picturesque arrangement and the chimneys sent up clouds of blue wood-smoke, giving a delicious scent to the air. It is true that more visitors were beginning to come into the district, but it was mostly in the summer; and those who came appreciated the emptiness and charm as compared with the crowded sands and promenades of the bigger Devon seaside towns, while the living expenses in the country remained at a comparatively lower level long after they had risen in more populated parts. In fact many people considered life in the South Hams to be a hundred years behind the times right up to World War I.

Agriculture has always been the main industry in the South Hams and some farms have been in the same family for generations. Farmhouses tended to follow a set pattern, in construction if not in plan. Many, chiefly those built before the middle of the nineteenth century, had the lower part of their walls made of huge stones above which the walls continued upwards in cob, that age-old mixture of earth, straw and a few pebbles or gravel. The roof was often of thatch, either straw or locally grown reeds, though local slate was also much in evidence, especially in the villages. A cheap and easy way of repairing damage to an inside cob wall was to take a loaf of bread, soak it in water and then stuff it into the hole, plaster it over and either whitewash or paper it! Though not encouraged, it was certainly done on occasions and, as a repair, what's more, it lasted. Many old cob walls can still be seen today.

One rather charming and unusual way of dividing up the fields, particularly round Stokenham and Chillington, was by using slabs of slate known as 'the Shiners', from a nearby quarry (plate, page 33). They were put into the ground in an upright position thereby making a most formidable barrier to almost any grazing animal. Regrettably they have been removed in many places now, though the immediate surroundings of Stokenham Church can still show a few in the hedges. The reason for removal seems to be twofold. In one case the fields thus constructed were said to be too small economically, but another explanation was that time and weather had worn the edges of these soft slates, causing the crevices between them to show such tempting views of the field on the other side of the fence that several sheep had tried to squeeze through, had fallen, and were later found dead, with broken legs.

Life was calmer, slower and very regular on the farm in those days. Food was simple but wholesome, and animals led a natural existence. Every farmyard, for instance, had poultry scratching around in happy occupation all day long. Poultry-keeping was the way that a farmer's wife would hope to make extra money, and the weekly trip to the nearest market with good fresh eggs, cream and butter and the occasional table bird was of as much importance to her as the cattle were to 'maister'. At Christmas, big consignments of turkeys and chicken were sent all over Devon and sometimes further afield.

While the men's work in the fields, orchards and woods was going on, the farmer's wife had plenty to occupy her. The rich milk from those South Devon herds, some of the best in the whole country, had to be put to good and immediate use. Any surplus left over after the daily local delivery had to be used at once, for the sheer kindness of the climate would not allow any to stand about, especially in high summer. It had long been the practice in various parts of the southern counties to dig what was known as an ice-house, deep down in the cool earth, where perishable goods could be safely kept for a few days. But the South Hams version was a 'butter house'. Choosing a spot under trees for preference, a little shelter or hut was constructed over a running stream which had been diverted from a bigger flow of water—of which there is much in that part of the country. The farmer's wife, having set to work and made butter, cheese and, best of all, the famous clotted cream, ready for market or local consumption, popped the result into the cool butter house.

When separating machines were invented they were hand-turned but were soon adapted to electricity, though they were not always welcome. One old woman described the machine as 'that chicksey-pixie 'ol trade'—an eloquent piece of Devon dialect. The machine quickly divides the cream from milk and the cream can then be scalded—clotted cream. But the correct and old-fashioned westcountry method is to stand new milk in a shallow pan for a few hours for the cream to rise to the surface. This pan is then lifted gently into a bigger pan containing water, and the whole is simmered over a slow heat until the cream forms a 'blanket'. Again, gently lifted, the pan is put into a cool place for a few hours, then the crust of scalded or clotted cream is carefully skimmed off. This works best with rich milk such as that from Red Devon, South Devon or Channel Islands cattle.

Market day was the real weekly outing and then the farmer and his 'missus' would get off to an early start in the horse and cart, though on occasion he might be driving a herd or flock to be sold and that would be a much slower process. But with his well-trained dog and perhaps a boy to help him he would get on well enough. If, on these occasions, 'maister' should arrive home a little 'market-merry' as the saying was, no one was surprised for, after all, was not cider one of Devon's most noted products?

People mostly moved around by horse-drawn vehicles or on horseback. The traditional stage-coach was still running for some time after other parts of the country had discontinued the custom and one of these stage-coaches was still to be seen in the yard of an inn at Kingsbridge in the early twenties of this century. But for those who had no such means there was the local carrier who often penetrated deep into the countryside, linking up isolated farms, hamlets and market towns. In the very old days the covered horse-drawn van had a wooden seat each side so that the passengers sat looking at each other. Sometimes the floor was covered with straw, especially in winter, and that served the double purpose of keeping the feet warm and the floor clean. A small oil lamp hung in one corner to give a gleam of light on dark evenings. The driver would be a well known character who would cheerfully undertake any reasonable shopping for those unable to make the journey into the market town; he would have regular and recognised stopping places but would always pull up if a prearranged signal was shown over a garden gate or from a cottage window. Later, of course, all this traffic was taken over by local buses. If the local bus services of today continue to be curtailed or even discontinued, as some have been, then it might be a good idea to start a modernised version of the village carrier again! For even today not everyone can own or drive a car.

The packhorse trade, the ancient method of selling goods in rural areas, was still quite a flourishing one in the early part of the twentieth century—it was, indeed, a very useful and paying business. There were regular customers who would be only too glad to buy from these itinerant sellers and thereby save themselves the journey into the nearest town. In the 1920s and 1930s, the packhorse became not so much a pony ridden by a man with a pack on his back or across the saddle as it once was, but would more likely be a pony- or donkey-cart which would be filled with the particular commodities in which the owner specialised. He would have regular 'rounds' and his customers would be on the look out for him. He might offer general merchandise, kitchen hardware, or blankets and linen for the linen cupboard; a fish cart might come from the coast; or a woman might come round offering haberdashery such as needles and threads, or knitting wools and so on. In springtime, a cart full of bedding plants might make the odd journey or two from the country to the local town with geraniums or lobelias and suchlike popular varieties to sell to the owners of the little town gardens who had no means, or the time, for raising seedlings for themselves. All these vendors would be well known, respected and recommended by one householder to another. Incidentally, the sea-kale which grows wild on Slapton Sands was first cultivated for kitchen use by a Mr Southcote of Stoke Fleming in the 1770s, roots of it being sold in Exeter market at 2s 6d (12½p) (30c) each. It was also possible to have specially ordered articles brought direct from a warehouse and, right into the beginning of this century, it was not unknown for the old packhorse custom to be followed occasionally by big town firms who, even between the wars, would send a man in a van to the country home of a valued customer with a large selection of goods as requested. This only happened rarely of course and the customer needed to be very privileged! The daughter of the house might buy household linens or other items for her trousseau in this way, though World War II, and the more general use of the motor car, soon swept away these more leisurely methods of shopping.

With so much horseflesh about in those days there had to be blacksmiths or farriers who not only shod the horses and ponies brought to the forge, but who also repaired ironwork on agricultural machinery and tools. They would fashion bolts and window fastenings, make gates and implements for the kitchen, or 'irons' for the parlour fireplace; they were real craftsmen, ready to turn their knowledge and experience to any problem brought to them. Although there are not enough horses about now to keep a skilled farrier really busy, his craft has by no means been allowed to die out. There are always discerning people who like handmade articles and who will order wrought-iron gates, lamps, fenders and decorations of all kinds; also there are many types of garden tools which can be mended by local men. Farriers were much in demand right up to World War II and there is still hunting to be had with the South Pool harriers not far from Slapton Sands, which means there is still some need for their skill.

Out of an old book bought in an auction sale some time ago there fluttered a little newspaper cutting containing the following delightful poem. There is no date on the cutting but it was obviously taken from a local paper and was probably published between the wars. It reads:

Thousands of horseshoes I have made
Both large and small
And hung them on the wall.
On horses and ponies I've nailed them all.
My anvil is worn
And my bellows torn;
My hammers and sledge lay on the floor
I made out the fire
And said it's time to retire;
I locked up the door and did no more.

Edward Jarvis
blacksmith of Slapton
(on his retirement)

To show how hardworking as well as isolated in their peaceful lives some of the inhabitants of the South Hams were, one can cite the story of the two men who, after much talk, decided to take advantage of the Great Western Railway's day excursion to London, at a sum which would arouse envy, if not actual disbelief, today. This was a great adventure; neither had ever been out of Devon before, as farm labourers (as agricultural workers were called then) had little opportunity to take holidays. First they had to make an early start to drive to Kingsbridge station, a matter of some miles; then they had to change at South Brent to join the excursion train from Plymouth. The brief stops at Newton Abbot and Exeter to pick up more passengers provided interesting distractions; the country was discussed and commented upon all the way with great interest until finally the train arrived at Paddington station which was large, crowded and noisy. The two men found the bustle very entertaining even if slightly bewildering, so they just stood and watched for a while. Then, feeling thirsty, they discovered the Refreshment Room and repaired thither to sample London's beer.

Some time later, still full of wonder and surprise, they decided to stay there and have a meal, and it was not until late in the afternoon that they felt it about time to look at London. So, feeling thoroughly adventurous, they ventured forth and stood for a while in Praed Street, amazed at the traffic and hum and bustle of the big city. They decided that 'Lunnon was a turrible big place' and, rather than risk losing touch with the railway station, they turned back. From then on they spent the rest of the time before the train started its return trip in happy, slightly mellow contemplation of the now familiar Refreshment Room. What their friends thought and said of the expedition when it was related to them a day or so later in the village pub would have been interesting to hear.

There was also a very pleasant social life at a different level to be found round and about the South Hams. The district contained, as it still does, some big and delightful country houses, often with semi-tropical trees, shrubs and plants in their gardens, the climate being so mild. Charming homes in the villages or high up on the hillsides all seemed, as indeed they do now, to add to the beauty and peace. Those with a view of the sea had the best of both worlds, though unfortunately a beautiful cliff-side garden at Blackpool Sands suffered a landslide in the early days of this century, which destroyed many rare and beautiful trees and plants. The disaster was blamed on the fact that a quantity of sand and gravel, much in demand by construction firms, had been dredged out of the sea only just offshore for some time past, leaving a depression in the sandbank. A worse example of erosion occurred in 1917 when a huge bank of shingle was removed from about two miles off Hallsands, just south of Torcross, to help in the construction of a new breakwater at Plymouth harbour. When the next gale came this vacuum filled with a gigantic wave which swept wildly inshore, up the beach, and completely engulfed the little fishing village of about twenty cottages. Even those cottages which were built higher up in the cliffs were affected, but happily no lives were lost. The village was never inhabited again, save by one occupant, the daughter of a fisherman. She had been born in the cottage, up on the cliff, which had always been her home, and soon after the disaster she returned to live alone, the only occupant of this ghost village. There she stayed until her death in 1970.

When World War I began it brought the first real changes that the South Hams had seen for centuries. The young men disappeared into the forces and many young women went away too, for there was much they could do in hospitals, Voluntary Aid Detachment, munition factories and other ways of taking men's places in civilian life. At first, life in this out-of-the-way spot continued much as before. Food was short of course, though the farmers did their best to keep supplies going; but soon there were moments of tragedy when news came through that there were those who would never come home again, and blue-clad wounded soldiers were to be seen even in this secluded spot, convalescing in the good South Devon air. During this period the large house in Slapton village which had been built in the grounds of the ruined Chantry, was being run as a guest house by a wounded, discharged Belgian soldier and his English wife. One summer such a big party of guests arrived that many had to sleep out in adjoining cottages. So many visitors all at once had never been seen in the village before and they afforded much speculation and amusement among the local inhabitants —especially as one young woman, anticipating fashion by a good forty years, removed shoes and stockings to walk down the muddy village street in a downpour of rain. Disapproval was registered in this case.

The south of England was by then full of Belgian refugees escaping from the Germans, and it was with that in mind that an unprecedented event took place in the little village hall during that summer. A group of young people from the guest house contrived to stage a shortened version of Laurence Housman's *Prunella*. How the costumes were devised, the parts learned and the play produced in the time available was due not only to the efforts of the group but to the encouragement of some older, theatrically-minded people also staying in the guest house. One of the girls had recently been in a school production of the same play and that had sparked off the idea. The little village hall was packed, and the resulting door money was duly presented to the Belgian Relief Fund. What the audience made of the show is not recorded, but if the rapt attenion which was given to it counts for anything it must have been a great success.

Nevertheless, war or no war, there was still time for picnics and such expeditions as going by carrier as far as Strete and then walking back again along the beautiful road by the Sands and, as the younger guests were quick to discover, a pony or two could also be hired for the day. One picnic was planned as a jaunt to Lannacombe, a delightful and, in those days, unfrequented beach to the south of Torcross and not far from Start Point. The ponies were ridden in turns by some of the party, while in addition a donkey-cart was available to carry the picnic basket and the youngest members of the group. All went well until the return journey when the skies turned grey and sullen, a few drops of rain fell, then down it came in cascades as a real summer storm. 'Hurry, hurry', cried the pony riders and most of the party took their advice, but the donkey saw no reason whatever to hasten his steps. He was accustomed to a slow plod and the girl who was leading him and trying to urge him along, not to mention the children huddled inside the cart, had perforce to suffer the slowest crawl imaginable along the gale-driven road. One or two kindly minded grown-ups stayed with the equipage to suffer the stinging rain coming over the sea, and one was heard to mutter 'Now I know what "stubborn as a donkey" means'.

Another member of that house-party, a rather august elderly lady, spent one afternoon alone in the adjoining ruined tower, emerging later to say that she had been conversing with Father Ignatius, known as the 'grey monk'. This monastic character was reputed to haunt the forbidding looking tower, but no one was brave enough, or perhaps interested enough, to ask her what their conversation had been about. This tower dominates Slapton village and yet it has but a short history. Known as the 'Chantry', it was built as part of a collegiate college in December 1372 but was dissolved 170 years later in November 1545. The *History of Slapton Church,* reprinted from the *Exeter Diocesan Gazette,* mentions a dispute over a demand for a subscription to the king's supremacy of the Church. The tower was left but the rest of the building was pulled down and the big house, which was being used as the guest house in 1917, was built in the grounds. Having survived many owners it has recently been turned into flats.

An activity which did have a long history in the South Hams was sea fishing although over the years it had declined a little, the busiest fishermen being those who dealt in shell-fish; certainly crab and lobster pots were always in evidence on the beaches to the south of the Limpet rocks at Torcross. Shoals of mackerel and other fish still occasionally came near the shore, however, and after World War I a man who had been badly wounded and was staying for a time at Torcross, although unable to walk, could crawl somehow down the shingle, enter the sea and swim, which he did daily. During one summer the shoals of mackerel were so plentiful that he found himself in the midst of them one day and, making a bet with friends that he could catch one in his bare hands, he set out the next morning to fulfil his boast. The fish were certainly there as all could see by the ripple of water and the occasional jump, not to mention the noisy seagulls who were also after the tiny brit, the mackerel's prey. After an interval the man gave a shout and held up a good-sized mackerel to show to those on the shingle. He brought it ashore, it was duly admired and shown around, and a rewarding glass was handed to this unconventional fisherman. It was not until some time later that he confessed that he had a concealed fishing line under his bathing costume—in those days such garments covered more than could the modern trunks!

When the war finished the countryside settled down again much as before, its beauty unimpaired, its peace even more appreciated. The sad gaps in family life had in time to be accepted and those who were maimed gradually learned to fit into the world again as best they could, while the good farming way of life continued as though the interruption of war had never been. In the early twenties motor cars were becoming commonplace and although they occasionally annoyed the horse traffic or the man driving livestock along the road, it quickly became the custom for the car to stop to allow them to go by, a wave of the hand following in acknowledgement. The main roads themselves looked different in those days for the more modern method of dressing the surface unfortunately gives a dark appearance, which country people used to say made night travelling more hazardous. Hitherto, until such time as the traction engine came into use, any main road, as distinct from the grassy lanes, was built up with stone pounded into place by hand tools and 'stonecracker John' was a familiar sight. Employees of the local county councils, such men would sit by the roadside with heaps of great stone blocks, their task being to break these up with a hammer into small bits suitable for repairing the roads. They wore protective eyeglasses and when one group of blocks was finished they would be moved away, sometimes many miles, to the next group dumped where the road needed mending.

This pounded stone did result in a 'white' road, although the dust it gave off, particularly in the summer, was not always welcome. However, in the words of the poet, 'the road was a ribbon of moonlight', and that is exactly what one young woman found when she rode out on her pony one beautiful moonlight night from Torcross to Kingsbridge to attend some gathering. At that time all telephone wires were carried by high poles along the roadside for there was no underground wiring system in that part of Devon: on this particular occasion the moonlight threw heavy black shadows from these poles right across the road and the pony insisted upon jumping over every single one. He only gave a little hop but it continued for miles much to the amusement of his rider and apparently to his own enjoyment too.

It would be impossible to give any description of the South Hams without mentioning one of its most interesting features—Slapton Ley, today a nature reserve. This is a freshwater lake running parallel with the sea for two and a half miles between Strete Gate and Torcross. There are other freshwater lakes by the sea, fed by streams from the hills, and some of these are close at hand, but Slapton Ley is the largest and also the most

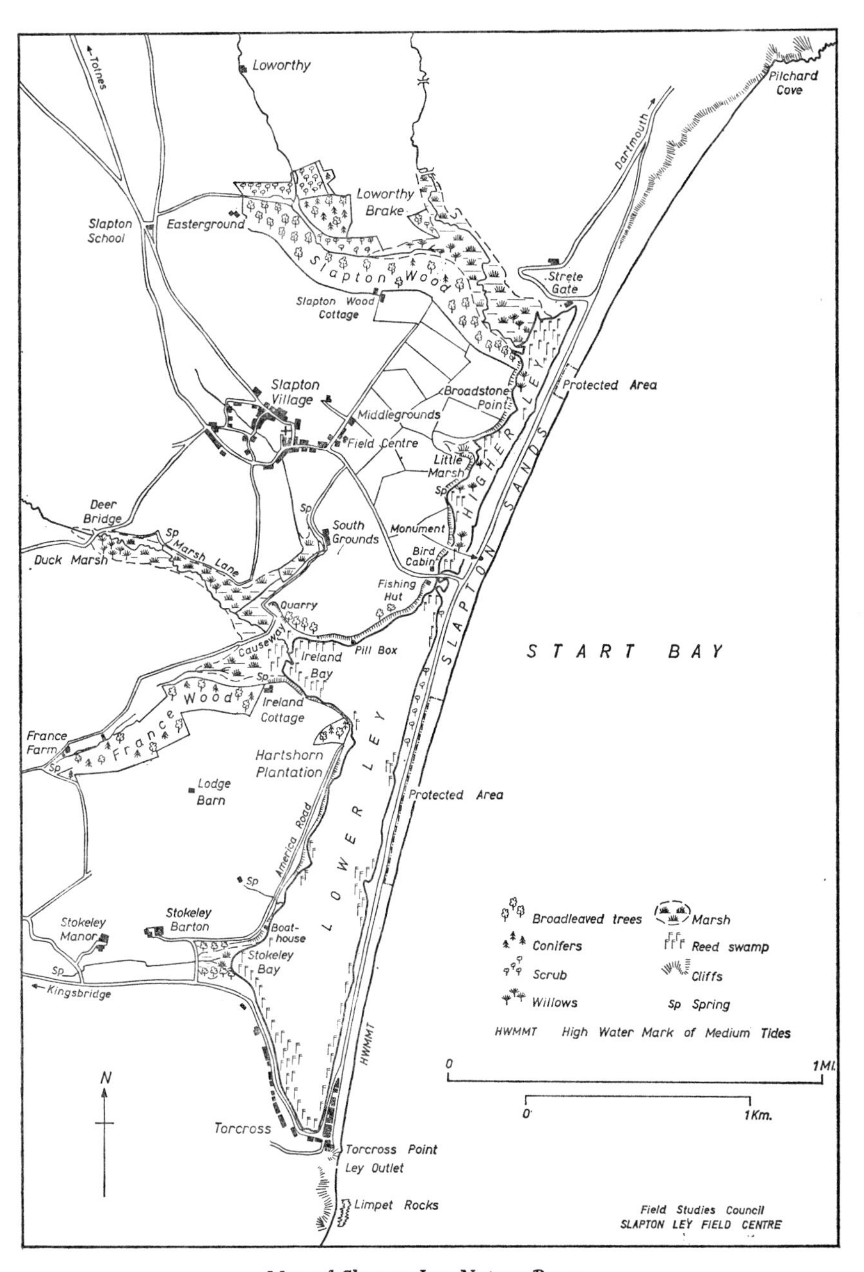

Map of Slapton Ley Nature Reserve

important from the wild life point of view. John Leland, who made his famous journey through England in the sixteenth century, wrote that 'Ther is but a Barre of Sande betwixt the Se and this Poole' and broadly speaking that is a good description, though there is now quite a width of grass verge as well beside the straight road which is all that separates the sloping beach from the lake along the latter's entire length. This road was a packhorse trail originally but in 1856 was constructed as a well-built turnpike road. Two years after the road was finished a coach service ran between Dartmouth and Kingsbridge and continued until the middle of World War I. The fare in the early days of this century was 2s (10p) (25c). At the same time proper provision was made for the overflowing of the Ley by constructing a big culvert at the Torcross end, which leads the surplus water underground to drain quietly away into the sea. The turnpike house, now turned into a charming cottage, stands just outside Torcross on the Stokenham side, opposite the turning into Stretely Manor; and the road running between the sea and the Ley before being properly constructed was reported to have been made up of 'crushed scallop shells, bundles of reeds, shingle and anything else handy'.

The Ley is fed by the Gara river and three smaller streams but is nowhere deeper than 10 feet. Before the construction of the culvert the fresh water sometimes overflowed its banks, ran across the road and down the ridged shingle beach to join the sea, but this very rarely happens today. Even more rarely does the Ley freeze. Conversely, very occasionally, the sea has been known to rise over the road during a really formidable gale and enter the fresh water. When this has happened it has resulted in some of the freshwater fish in the Ley being killed. This interesting stretch of water has attracted naturalists for many decades and in the nineteenth century several well-known writers made notes of the wild life which abounded in the neighbourhood, not only in the Ley but also in the narrow lanes. Legend says, incidentally, that, when a few hundred years ago some of these lanes were given stones to lift them out of the mud there was a distinct outcry among some people, the complaint being that they were not only hard on the feet of the inhabitants but they were hard on the horses too.

In the 1930s there is no doubt that the well made-up road beside the Ley was hard on the feet of two locally well known but not very young men who decided over a jolly glass that they would run a race along the road, one insisting that, in spite of his age, he could show his friend a clean pair of heels from Torcross to the Royal Sands Hotel about halfway along, a distance of about a mile. So the wager was taken on and half the population of Kingsbridge turned out to see the race, lining the road on both sides and shouting encouragement and advice. One of the contestants had to give in just before the end of the course but the crowd still yelled to the front man 'go on—he's only just behind you', causing the poor winner to make further and quite unnecessary efforts—a feat still talked of today.

This Royal Sands Hotel stood opposite the Ley right on the edge of the shingle beach and was one of the best known buildings in the South Hams district. It was capacious, interesting and had the distinction of being called the 'Royal' Sands Hotel as the result of a call by King Edward VII when he was in the district visiting the Royal Naval College at Dartmouth. The bar had some very large glass cases hanging on its walls, containing some of the amazingly big carp caught in the Ley; there were also stables, for in days gone by the stage coach used to make it one of its regular stops. Another interesting visitor was a small steamship which paid regular visits to the hotel, bringing summer visitors on afternoon trips, and a delightful little jaunt it must have been. They landed on the shingle when it was calm enough by means of a portable landing stage.

The old bridge which crossed over the Ley and led to Slapton village was destroyed during World War II at the same time as the Royal Sands Hotel and the three lime kilns which stood nearby. A modern bridge was built as soon as possible but it is a wider version of the little narrow one which had stood there for many centuries, giving access to the packhorse trail along the coast long before the turnpike road was built. The early bridge could take a car but nevertheless it was very unobtrusive, especially in the dark, a fact which led to an amusing incident one night between the two wars. For one Christmas Eve, a merry party of young men decided to spend an evening at the hotel on the beach instead of, for once, patronising their own 'local'. So down the hill they clattered and remained in the bar until closing time, which was later than usual owing to the festive season. It was extremely dark when they got outside but they were much too happy to bother about that as they joked and sang and made their way to the little bridge. But they could not find it! They were all too 'mazed' to be systematic about a search, far too confused and far too gay, and after staggering up and down each way several times they confessed themselves lost. At that moment a man who worked at the hotel came along on his way home. He heard the raucous laughter and general rumpus and, knowing who they were, shouted out to ask what the trouble was. 'Us can't find bridge', came the answer from three or four voices all at once. After more laughter the young men formed a crocodile by hanging on to each other's shoulders and, with their rescuer at the head, soon found themselves across the bridge and on the way uphill. And their leader was a blind man! How could he tell in this pitch darkness where the bridge was when the others could not? The answer is that he went up and down the road every day, counting his steps in the beginning but later relying on instinct to guide him. A classic case of the blind leading the blind if there evere was.

Page 33 (above) *Aerial view of Slapton showing the Ley and surrounding countryside;* (below) *shiners—a local but fast-disappearing way of dividing fields with slabs of locally quarried slate—many of which were damaged during the Occupation*

Page 34 (above) *Mrs Ethel Mitchelmore and her son packing their belongings;* (below) *clearing a cottage at Slapton*

The Ley is much enjoyed by early swallows who find plenty of insect food in the reeds, and great clouds of starlings are to be seen at times too, flying in what appear to be highly organised manoeuvres. The reeds are also the home of many species of insects. These reeds were often used for fences as well as for thatching and the story goes that in medieval times they were cut for writing pens until it was discovered that birds' quills were more lasting and satisfactory. Fish abound in the Ley. Pike, perch, rudd and roach can always find plenty of food there to keep them alive and, on the waterline in the spring, there are nestling ducklings, coot and moorhens—all tasty little morsels for such predators as the big pike. These pike can reach a weight of well over 30lb and more.

Some amazing catches have been reported by anglers over the years, not only recording the sizes of the big pike but also huge numbers of other varieties. Impressive though some of the records are, perhaps they were not a much greater feat than that of some local boys who, strictly poaching, landed one of the really enormous pike for which the Ley is famous. The fishing between the two wars was private and a water bailiff was employed to see that it was kept so, but he could not be everywhere at once so that if a group of boys posted one of their number as a 'lookout' the others could happily dangle their lines and usually achieve a little success. Later on the property belonged to the Whitley Trust which allowed day tickets to those staying in the Royal Sands Hotel, and anglers would come for a few days simply to have the pleasure of trying their luck in this big freshwater expanse. Cautious poaching still went on, however, and one day a boy, with two or three friends, was happily engaged in pitting his skill against experienced fishermen when he suddenly had a bite. Now, his tackle consisted of a wriggling worm for bait as a substitute for a small live fish, and an 'S' hook from a butcher's shop bent over at one end to form a loop to which a good rope, borrowed from a farmyard and to be carefully returned again after use, was firmly attached. But on this occasion the boy was nearly dragged into the water. His friends came to help, bracing themselves against a convenient fence and at last, performing a real parabola, the pike, flying through the air over the heads of his captors, landed with a thud on the pathway behind. All this had taken time and no one had been on the lookout so it was with a shock that the boys heard a quiet voice saying 'Well, I'm damned; so that's how you do it! I can't even get a touch though I've got the most expensive equipment obtainable.'

This then was the South Hams at the end of the 1930s; still a bit behind the times but a happy, beautiful part of the world in which to live. No one could foresee how abruptly the way of life of the people in one particular part of it would come to an end in the winter of 1943.

TWO
The Order to Evacuate

BUT ALTHOUGH THE SOUTH HAMS ENJOYED ITS PEACE and plenty, comparatively untroubled by events of the world outside, as the 1930s advanced the politicians watched the international scene with increasing anxiety. Hitler rose to power and by 1938 Austria and Czechoslovakia had been made part of the German Reich. However, at a meeting at Munich in September 1938 between Neville Chamberlain, the British Prime Minister, and Hitler, it was agreed that Germany should leave Poland unmolested. Nevertheless, Britain's preparations for a possible war continued and Chamberlain declared publicly that, 'After Munich our defence programme was actually accelerated and expanded so as to remedy certain weaknesses which had become apparent during the crisis.' In fact, in the summer of 1938, when war seemed imminent, a military exercise took place in the South Hams when Brigadier Bernard Montgomery (later to be Field Marshal Viscount Montgomery of Alamein) took up his headquarters on Slapton Sands between the Royal Sands Hotel and Strete Gate and organised a large military landing exercise.

It was such a success that *The Times* newspaper reported on 8 July that the operation was to occupy five days but those concerned had done so well that it was completed in one! It was almost a dress rehearsal for the tremendous exercises which were carried out in exactly the same spot six years later but then under the strictest war conditions, including live ammunition.

The Munich agreement proved valid for only twelve months. On 1 September 1939 Germany moved into Poland to whom France and Great Britain had pledged help in the event of German aggression. On 3 September, Britain was at war. In Neville Chamberlain's words, 'It is a sad day for all of us. For none it is sadder than for me. Everything that I worked for, everything that I had hoped for, everything that I believed in during my public life has crashed into ruins this morning.' His words had far more personal significance for the people in the South Hams than they could realise that day.

On the very first day of the war, a general call-up of all men between eighteen and forty-one was announced, so that remote rural areas entered the war from the very beginning. Soon, rationing of food began to be proposed, though it was not finally brought in until early in 1940. Clothes were rationed from 2 June 1941 and this state of affairs continued until 1949. In 1942 sweets were rationed as well as soap. All over the country, farmers were encouraged to use every scrap of available land for the growing of food crops and for grazing but at the same time they were hampered by the call-up which took away so much agricultural labour. Only a few younger men were allowed to remain in order to help cope with the extra strain put upon the farms, and the Women's Land Army stepped into the breach almost at once. This by itself brought a sudden new look to the countryside. From the outbreak of war up to November 1939, 3,500 women received Land Army training at government expense, and were drafted into jobs as farm helpers in different parts of the country. By March 1943 that number had reached 58,221. Shipping bringing vital supplies of food and war materials to Britain from overseas suffered its greatest losses from enemy bombers, submarines and mines in the spring of 1943. Mr Hudson, Minister of Agriculture, appealed to the farmers everywhere to concentrate on grain, potatoes, milk and sugar beet; also that a further one million acres be ploughed up in addition to the appeal at the outbreak of war when the government offered £2 an acre for turning up grassland. In 1944 the total area of crops other than grass amounted to 14½ million acres which was 5¾ million acres more than in 1939, in spite of rural land being taken over for various kinds of war establishments such as aerodromes, etc. Another innovation which brought a fresh look to farming lands was the rapid increase in the number of tractors, of which the South Hams had its share. In 1939 the number of tractors in use over the whole country was 56,000 but by January 1946 that had increased to 203,000.

Another very early problem which rural areas had to deal with was the surge of evacuees who arrived in numbers both great and small. Every part of the British Isles was affected by this as those from the big towns and cities and from exposed positions on the coasts tried, indeed were encouraged, to get away as quickly as possible. People came not only as families or individuals but also in parties—schools, nursing homes, colleges and so on; in fact one school from Acton, London, turned up in a small South Devon town three days before war was declared and was welcomed by locally organised billeting officers who found room for all. The official number of government sponsored evacuees was 1,200,000 by the end of the war and the impact on rural South Devon of such 'foreigners' with their urban way of life was sometimes a little surprising.

On 6 September 1939 the first enemy aircraft arrived off the east coast of England but turned back before British fighters could make contact. This made the population realise that war in the air was going to be very different this time from that of World War I. Enemy planes soon began to attack Britain in increasing numbers—even the South Hams had its quota of tip and run raids. The planes would skim low over the sea then run in and drop the odd bomb with the general idea of demoralising the inhabitants, for even small hamlets and little villages were given their share of attention. One Home Guard in the South Hams, in charge of an anti-aircraft gun, had the chance of a lifetime as an enemy plane flew straight across his hidden post. 'It was an absolute sitting duck', he said afterwards, but he became so nervous and excited that he managed to jam his thumb round the trigger mechanism, so that the gun refused to fire. It took him a long time to get over that disappointment.

In 1940, the war in France was going badly; the Maginot Line had been broken, Paris had capitulated and, while the enemy was spreading over the countryside of France, the War Cabinet recalled British troops from Dunkirk. Although the town was under constant attack for a whole week, 335,490 officers and men were successfully brought back to England, the operation made possible by a vast collection of mixed vessels from warships to fishing boats and many ships made several trips. Two officers at home on a few days' leave got out a private yacht, sailed to the beaches, picked up the nearest soldiers, landed them ashore in England, berthed the yacht, and returned to their unit just as their leave was up! One man reported that he had been on the beach at Dunkirk for four days, helping wounded aboard, and that when finally he was offered a trip back in a substantial and seaworthy fishing smack he climbed aboard, sat down in a coil of anchor chains, fell asleep immediately and remained so for nearly the whole journey across the Channel. The weather that week was as kind and helpful as the weather for D Day in 1944 was to be terrible and obstructive. The south coast now became full of troops; wives, mothers and sweethearts from all parts of the country rushed down to greet them, and everybody opened their homes to this rescued, exhausted army.

But not all came home, for there were sick, wounded and dying men who could not possibly make the journey. In a few camp sick bays or hospitals in France, certain staff were detailed to stay behind to look after their patients when the rest were evacuated, and one of the saddest doctors who came back to Devon in that mammoth transfer was one of those who had originally been scheduled to remain with those who had to be left behind. At the very last moment orders were changed and he was put on the list for evacuation—he said he felt like a deserter. But this was no time for arguing. The group he was with were only just leaving a village as the enemy was heard advancing over the hills behind; one man told with great cheerfulness how he had escaped the notice of a machine-gunning enemy plane by ducking into a hen house and so remained, nicely hidden, until the enemy passed!

Once the escape of so many from Dunkirk was over, people in the South Hams, like those in the rest of the country, began to feel an increased pressure of war. There were air-raid casualties, much sickness, especially among the elderly, while the Civil Defence, Observer Corps, the Home Guard (affectionately known nowadays as 'Dad's Army') and other organisations like the Women's Voluntary Service did all they could to watch, to warn, to give any help they could, in conditions that became increasingly hard as time wore on.

By early 1943, however, the Allies were beginning to look forward towards an offensive into Europe and, in the spring of that year, a new Anglo-American staff was set up to help with the already existing plan to re-enter Normandy. The stretches chosen for the landing lay between Caen and the eastern beaches of the Cotentin Peninsula. It was decided that, if the proposed invasion was to have any chance of success, troop training under war conditions was absolutely necessary so that, in the heat of actual battle not only would each group know exactly what to do but when to do it. The training would apply not only to the assault troops themselves but also to the many others necessary to back them up. Nine training grounds were considered necessary and this is where a part of the South Hams entered active war life—becoming one of the nine. The beaches from Blackpool Sands to Torcross had already had the experience of the exercise in 1938 so that a certain amount of knowledge had already been acquired, and the group here was to undergo training in assault landings.

The planning staff calculated that the enemy would expect, if an Allied invasion were to come, that the troops would undoubtedly try to land in various harbours, as big troop-carrying vessels could not possibly come sufficiently inshore to drop men on the beaches. Therefore, argued the War Office, the enemy-held harbours would be heavily protected and, later, this was proved to be so. But to deceive the enemy and yet to get the Allied troops ashore, artificial harbours would have to be constructed. Not only was this one of the best-kept secrets of the war, but it was also one of the most successful efforts made in the struggle for peace; it was known as 'Operation Mulberry'. The scheme was to consist of an immense system of breakwaters, piers and concrete caissons. Two of these harbours were to be made: Mulberry 'A' for the American sector and Mulberry 'B' for the British. The risks attached to such a plan were great and there was no time or opportunity to experiment but nevertheless the joint staff decided to go ahead. An embryonic idea had already been worked upon so that the staff was able to complete their plan by the end of 1943 and, although alterations were then made, it was finalised by early 1944.

In order to accommodate the necessary amount of shipping and harbour equipment, each Mulberry had to be about the size of the harbour at Dover, and perhaps the biggest job was to make the 150 caissons. These were constructed in various places all over the country, the majority in Thames shipyards which employed some 20,000 workers in this part of the scheme alone. The caissons were to be dropped in shallow water and be protected by floating blockships. Floating piers to ride up and down with the tide completed the scheme.

Meanwhile, in further preparation for the invasion of France, many narrow and twisting roads leading to harbours on the south coast had to be straightened—some altered out of all recognition—for speed to the ports would be vital once the invasion had begun. Also, in a wartime emergency, a straight road could be used as a landing ground for a plane. Many curious things happened during 1943 along the southern part of England; for instance twenty miles inland a heath was requisitioned and American troops built concrete bases to hold thousands of jerricans of petrol; this construction took nearly a year to complete. A few weeks before the invasion it was full of cans piled high and covered with tarpaulins, and would have been a wonderful target for the Luftwaffe had it come; but by now there had been much destruction of the enemy's air force in Northern France, also of its radio installations and shore batteries, so that its powers were very much curtailed.

By that time the enemy was relying on its secret weapon, the 'flying bomb' (though actually the first one did not land until exactly one week after D Day, reported by the Royal Observer Corps at Dymchurch in Kent) and during 1943 the powers of attack in Allied aircraft had been increasing. In fact the change-over from defensive to offensive offered many opportunities to the Allies—all of which gave mounting confidence in the proposed invasion of France planned for 1944. Although there was remorseless fighting ahead, and much destruction and unhappiness yet to come to the people at home from the 'flying bombs' and the loss of lives and shipping at sea, nevertheless, the tide was turning. It is not always realised, though, that had D Day not taken place when it did, it could have been just a matter of a few weeks before the 'flying bombs' would have been landing all along the south coast instead of only on the south east including London. Installations so far had only been set up along part of the northern French coast but preparations were practically ready for the whole of the south of England to be bombarded, from 'hell-fire' corner in the neighbourhood of Dover, down towards Cornwall. When the Allies landed in Normandy on D Day and had driven the Germans out of the territories they were occupying it was easy to see, from the half-constructed bomb emplacements, the line of attack which had been planned.

In January 1944 General Dwight D. Eisenhower arrived in England, bringing with him his own staff of officers and technicians; the invasion plans were now complete, the different training areas were put into action and the general was given supreme command.

Meanwhile the summer of 1943 declined into a wet autumn, and at the beginning of November curious rumours were circulating in one particular part of the South Hams. The grapevine reported that some official-looking men had arrived in a big car, had entered and looked round Blackawton school, making notes, obviously with permission; they also had a look at the church. Later their car took them to the village hall at Stokenham, which they also entered. None of this escaped the notice of the villagers and when notes were compared somebody stated that he had heard that they had come from the Devon County Council and one, he knew, was from Kingsbridge Rural

District Council. 'Why?' asked the gossips, and it was no time at all before an inspired guess suggested that more people were to be drafted into that part of Devon. 'Or even,' said one man, remembering the seaborne exercise of five years ago, 'perhaps more troops are coming to practice landings again.'

Slapton and Blackpool Sands, in company with all south-coast beaches, had been shut off to the public ever since the beginning of the war and given protection in case of possible landings. There were mines, masses of barbed wire and notices everywhere, while any little fishing boat, even a dinghy, could only put to sea if granted a permit. The forlorn appearance of Slapton Sands was already aggravated by the damage done to the hotel which, right on the sands, had been evacuated in 1939 at the outbreak of war. A local black-and-white farm dog, named Pincher, had succeeded in crawling under the barrier one day, had trodden on a mine and blown up a part of the building as well as himself. That lovely stretch of coastline was indeed looking shabby and neglected.

On 4 November 1943, the chairman of the Devon County Council, Sir John Daw, received a phone call from the War Cabinet, informing him that a specified area was to be immediately and totally evacuated and that the date fixed for the evacuation to be complete was 20 December. It was being requisitioned under the Defence Regulations and Compensation Act of 1939. Four days later the regional commissioner, Sir Hugh Elles, convened two meetings at the Castle, Exeter, to initiate the project of lending the Area to US troops to practice assault landings. Stationed in Bristol, he was responsible in the South West for any big civilian movements which might be directly or indirectly caused by the war, that is, either through enemy action or for any other reason.

The first meeting informed local councils and other voluntary groups of the timing and scope of the evacuation plans, and at this meeting the chairman of the county council pointed out that the terms of the 1939 Act would be inadequate to deal with the situation and that there would be nothing like enough transport to cope with the farm stock, agricultural equipment and household goods. These problems were already being considered by the government, said Sir Hugh Elles. He and his deputy, Mr Harper, a retired civil servant, were empowered to call on any civilian body for help when and where necessary, and the Royal Navy, which was to be in charge of the seaborne exercises, was to supply a number of maintenance men who would not only help staff the necessary information centres but would run a hostel, outside the Area, for the use of officials from the different ministries who would have to come to the district.

The second meeting was composed of clergy who served the neighbourhood due to be vacated. They were told that a total evacuation of 30,000 acres was to take place at once, involving parts of 6 parishes, 3,000 people, 180 farms, village shops and other dwellings, concerning 750 families in all. The area involved consisted of a triangle from Torcross to Blackpool Sands and stretching uphill to Blackawton at its apex. It included the villages of Torcross, Slapton, Strete, Blackawton, East Allington, Sherford, Stokenham and Chillington. All farm possessions, animals, agricultural machinery, household goods, indeed anything movable of any value, and as many crops still in the ground as could be saved, were all to be taken away. This enormous task had to be completed in six weeks. The clergy were also informed that the government promised to pay every expense in connection with the evacuation, would give all help in finding temporary accommodation, would pay rents, grant free storage during the period of absence, and that everything would be brought back under the same guarantee while any damage would be repaired and paid for. The clergy were also told that it would be necessary to start the scheme at once for the land was due to be handed over to the War Office on 20 December for troop training. They were asked to use their discretion as to whom they told at the moment, as the parishes in question were to be informed officially at special meetings within a few days. The Occupation was to last for about six months but it was pointed out that the inhabitants might not be able to return at once since a clearing-up operation would almost certainly be necessary. Having regard, though, to the value of the agricultural land involved, the greatest efforts would be made to reinstate the farmers as soon as possible.

On 12 November—a day after the memorial services for the Armistice of World War I—the Lord Lieutenant of Devon, Lord Fortescue, addressed a meeting held at East Allington church to explain the position to the people, namely that this particular part of the South Hams was to be used for practice for assault landings when a Second Front was opened. Later in the day he held another meeting at Stokenham church. Soft Devon rain was falling now, as it did for much of the next six weeks, all adding to the sadness of the bewildered and shocked people, many of whom had not even heard the rumours. They went quietly back to their homes to look at the familiar surroundings and to wonder 'for how long?' and 'shall we ever come back again?'. The next day Sir John Daw held similar meetings at Blackawton church and at Slapton village hall and the news was received in the same stunned fashion; all these meetings were also attended by Sir Hugh Elles. It was difficult for some to believe the shattering news, for the Area was richly agricultural and the need for home-grown food greater than ever. Many were at a loss to understand why such valuable land should be especially commandeered. Actually, though of course the War Office was not going into details, it was because there was a certain resemblance between the South Hams beaches and those in Normandy where troops were scheduled to land on D Day.

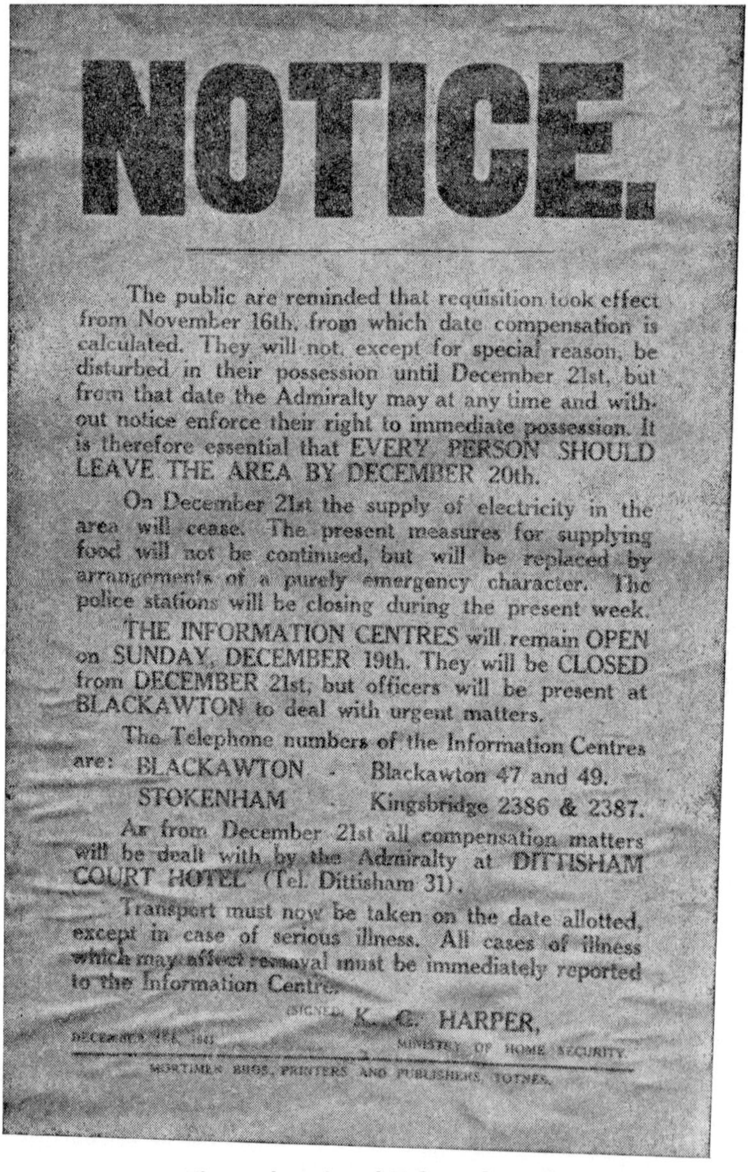

NOTICE.

The public are reminded that requisition took effect from November 16th, from which date compensation is calculated. They will not, except for special reason, be disturbed in their possession until December 21st, but from that date the Admiralty may at any time and without notice enforce their right to immediate possession. It is therefore essential that EVERY PERSON SHOULD LEAVE THE AREA BY DECEMBER 20th.

On December 21st the supply of electricity in the area will cease. The present measures for supplying food will not be continued, but will be replaced by arrangements of a purely emergency character. The police stations will be closing during the present week.

THE INFORMATION CENTRES will remain OPEN on SUNDAY, DECEMBER 19th. They will be CLOSED from DECEMBER 21st, but officers will be present at BLACKAWTON to deal with urgent matters.

The Telephone numbers of the Information Centres are:

BLACKAWTON -	Blackawton 47 and 49.
STOKENHAM -	Kingsbridge 2386 & 2387.

As from December 21st all compensation matters will be dealt with by the Admiralty at DITTISHAM COURT HOTEL (Tel. Dittisham 31).

Transport must now be taken on the date allotted, except in case of serious illness. All cases of illness which may affect removal must be immediately reported to the Information Centre.

(SIGNED) K. C. HARPER,

DECEMBER [illegible] 1943 — MINISTRY OF HOME SECURITY.

MORTIMER BROS., PRINTERS AND PUBLISHERS, TOTNES.

The proclamation of 11 December 1943

The Ministries of Transport, Labour, Food, Fuel & Power, Pensions and Agriculture were called upon to help, together with the Civil Defence, the Home Guard, the Royal Society for the Prevention of Cruelty to Animals, St John Ambulance Brigade, British Red Cross, Women's Voluntary Service, Voluntary Aid Detachment and other voluntary bodies. The Navy sent thirty photographers and surveyors to inspect and value every acre of land for reference when the occupation should be over.

At a meeting of the Devon County Council on 6 January 1944 the chairman, Sir John Daw, read a letter from Sir Hugh Elles dated 30 December 1943. It expressed admiration for the public-spirited manner in which the local people had responded to the demands made upon them, and placed on record his appreciation of the way in which the difficult task had been handled by the workers concerned. Major Rayner (later Brigadier Sir Ralph Rayner), MP for the Totnes Parliamentary division which included the area in question, had been given special leave to attend the meeting; he stated that he fully shared the view that the compensation under the Defence Act of 1939 would in no way be sufficient. The only course open to those who had the interests of the evacuees at heart would be to raise funds by an appeal for voluntary contributions.

So began a period of the greatest upheaval, the biggest disturbance that this part of the South Hams had ever known; followed by months of the worst neglect that the neighbourhood had ever experienced in all its history.

THREE
Exodus

MANY OF THE FARMERS, DEEP IN THEIR NORMAL DAILY work, were taken completely by surprise at the news of the Evacuation. One man who had been engaged most of the day with a difficult calving came indoors late in the afternoon and sank thankfully into his usual comfortable chair by the kitchen fire, wondering where his wife was on this dreary, wet afternoon. He suddenly remembered that she had spoken of some meeting in the village, hastily called together, the purpose not explained. However as he was taking off his boots, in she came, and one look at her face was enough to warn him of trouble to come.

'We've got to clear out', she said with trembling lips, and it was quite a time before he could really get the gist of her story. Even then he could scarcely believe it. Leave his farm and drop all the hard work he had put into growing extra food—at the behest of the government too—why, it was unbelievable. He bethought himself of the new calf and the rest of his stock—where to go and what to do with his well-organised life, all his

Page 51 (above) *A threshing plant being moved from a South Hams farm;* (below) *Herbert Read supervising the careful removal and packing of parts of the screen from Blackawton Church*

Page 52 (above) *WVS workers washing up outside the cowshed which was turned into an emergency kitchen during the evacuation;* (below) *Royal Sands Hotel, Slapton, too badly damaged during the assault to be rebuilt*

household possessions, his farm equipment and crops. 'Got to clear out?' he muttered. He gradually came to appreciate the reason, was one of the first to seek aid and accept the situation, but he never forgot that wet afternoon and the realisation that his life was to be as suddenly cut off as if he had been hit by a bullet. As for his wife, 'Er did cry and grieved terrible about it, but 'twas no use grieving—if you had to go that was that', was his attitude.

To move 3,000 people in a hurry from a town, a suburb or a modern housing estate would be a different story from doing so in the South Hams for, as we have seen, practically all the land there was, and still is, farmland. Emptying a house of its contents, unless it were a big mansion, would only be the matter of a day or two, but this evacuation meant everything movable, including animals, farmyard equipment and crops still in the ground. Moving the contents of a farmhouse sometimes required only a small proportion of the time spent in taking the outdoor equipment away, so that the transport problem became a Herculean task. But a man living just outside the area is reported to have said, 'Six weeks to clear out! Why, I was only given six hours—and I made it.' It appeared that his home had been in a particularly dangerous spot in another part of the country and that his exile was to last for the duration of the war. 'There's always someone worse off than yourself,' was the obvious, but sympathetic rejoinder of a bystander.

To provide focal points to which people could go for help, two Information Centres were set up, one in Blackawton and the other at Stokenham, and these were manned by the Women's Voluntary Service, who had an enormous list of helpers to rely upon. They came from Totnes, Dartmouth, Plympton, Newton Ferrers, Plymstock, Kingsbridge—to name but a few places; while many more came from further away as time went on and the need for assistance became even more pressing. Notices were posted up at once, telling people where to go for help and advice, and WVS members were sent to every dwelling in the area to make sure that everyone had heard the news and understood that they must make immediate plans to get away as quickly as possible. It had to be explained, over and over again, that it would be criminal to send troops to land in enemy-occupied country as frontline men without giving them some experience of what to expect. The organisers were at the Centres from 8.30 in the morning until 5, 6, or even 7 in the evening, in cold and sometimes difficult conditions. Often many people arrived together; a few would be deaf, or perhaps a little dim-witted so that they could not be made to understand the urgency. Just occasionally someone would be temporarily put out by the whole affair, and one or two were really cantankerous. Never had there been such a need for tact and persuasion, and the helpers were really called upon to give of their best. But there was so much to be done in such a short time that the atmosphere was mostly one of orderly bustle.

The first day at Stokenham, for instance, had an Alice-in-Wonderland air about it for the Navy, wishing to make sure that the electricity in the hall was up to their stringent requirements, requested the local electricity board to remove their wiring. So at one end of the room, a WVS worker said, a local man was busy taking out the existing wiring and directly he had finished, a naval rating, with a cheery word as he borrowed the ladder, put fresh wiring in its place. Such a good beginning, she thought. Then an enormous telephone switchboard was put in, and one of the first requests was to Lady Reading—the founder and head of the WVS—for as many boxes, crates and barrels of any size or description as she could possibly get hold of for distribution to the people, one of whose first anxieties was the lack of containers for packing. To the surprise and delight of the helpers, an enormous collection of such articles was put on the train and delivered to the Centre by lorry in such a short time that it was hardly believable. A human chain had to be formed at once to get the containers inside, and it amused some of the helpers very much to see everybody linked in the chain, for the job had to be done as quickly as possible, with no standing on dignity. These boxes were handed out to all who needed them at one shilling (5p) a time. The majority of the inhabitants were not used to moving about very much and had no experience of the wholesale packing that evacuation was going to mean; moreover the effect of the conscription call-up was making itself felt by now, which meant that many of the inhabitants were either over sixty-five or else were children.

The first questions asked in the Centres were almost routine: 'Where can we go?' 'What can we pack our things in? We haven't even got a suitcase.' 'What about our ration cards?' 'The whole of our winter's coal ration is in the shed—we shan't have to leave it behind shall we?' Many, in the early days of the Evacuation, seemed utterly appalled by the difficulties, but those with the greatest problems were the farmers with their stock and crops, fodder and all kinds of agricultural machinery. Many had to sell whole herds, and if a man had spent nearly a lifetime in building up a particular strain it was a heart-breaking business. Two special cattle sales were held at Kingsbridge, but after the second one it was realised that it would be useless to try any more as the local market had now been flooded. Frank R. Horne, who was at that time agricultural botanist at Seale Hayne Agricultural College, recalls being sent down during the exodus to help with advice over crop removal and other farming problems. He says that one of his clearest recollections is the amazing way in which many dairy herds and other animals were taken in and given a temporary home just outside the Area. Two or three fields and an unused barn were a godsend. In their efforts to help, many local farmers gave a home to so many cattle belonging to friends and neighbours that there had to be two milkings each morning and each evening to cope with the numbers. While the animals were out in the fields they grazed together without fuss but, when it came to milking time the residents went into the cowshed they had always used while the visitors learned to use another one—with no bother at all. Mr Horne stated, furthermore, that the affair aroused the warmest feelings of sympathy in what, he believes, is one of the most hospitable parts of the South Hams.

The WVS battled on, coping as best they could with the incessant phone calls and the demand for cars for both long and short journeys. Anyone requiring transport, whether to inspect a temporary home or just to make a quick run to the towns of Kingsbridge or Dartmouth, both just outside the Evacuation Area, to see a house agent, a solicitor, a bank manager or to deal with any other business connected with moving out was granted, free of charge, a car with a volunteer driver and enough petrol for the trip. One family actually visited five houses before they were satisfied. Private petrol was now completely cut off all over the country save for very special cases, and the price of a gallon of petrol at that time was 1s 10d (9p). Kingsbridge, in particular, found itself very much involved in many of the problems. Its Rural District Council normally controlled the part to be evacuated and its professional and business people were consulted on many occasions regarding matters which could not be dealt with by the voluntary helpers at the information Centres; though the latter were in touch by telephone with every organisation concerned. So the two Centres continued with the daily calls from the people; some requiring comforting, reassuring and encouragement, for the human element was one of the big considerations. The assistant regional commissioner said one day to a WVS organiser, 'Rules are rules and a government official can't break them—that is where the

WVS comes in.' Sympathy and understanding were much needed, but firmness and commonsense had to play their part too, though it was generally agreed that the acceptance of the position and the co-operation from the people was wonderful. In fact one of the most heart-warming aspects of the whole Evacuation was the quiet acceptance of the situation as demonstrated by so many after the initial shock was over. As one man put it, 'I said to the boy, I said, if it'll help our chaps out there fighting for us then us 'ave got to go.'

An able local man, who knew the neighbourhood like the back of his hand, was put in charge of the all-important transport; it was his task to summon a fleet of lorries, pantechnicons and vans from wherever they could be found—all over the country. His telephone had to be manned day and night, and he managed this by pressing members of his family into a rota. His was one of the most important and responsible tasks of the Evacuation and he worked entirely on a voluntary basis. Not only did it embroil all his family through telephone duty, but the difficulty of obtaining enough vehicles, especially in the early stages of the Evacuation, was alarming. As soon as the first commandeered vehicles arrived, petrol grants were issued and the vans despatched to the earliest outgoing households. It was soon found, however, that once a lorry was sent to a farm dwelling there was no telling when it would return again; one farm alone took five lorries in which to pack just the agricultural machinery and implements and another took a week in packing the outdoor stuff alone; then the distance to the family's new accommodation was not always known.

By now so much of the South West was filled with evacuees from the more densely populated towns and cities that the villages could take no more. So, although the nearby countryside did its best, especially with regard to the farmers, private people in the area often had to go far away to find a new home. In fact one woman was quite gleeful when relations invited her to stay with them in Scotland, as she had always wished to visit them but had never been able to afford the railway journey! This being granted to her, she departed, the furniture followed and she was never seen again.

One of the greatest headaches was caused by the little lanes which were such a beautiful feature of that part of South Devon in summer. They were, in many cases, grass-grown tracks, and very muddy in winter, and once a heavy lorry or two had run the length of the lane it was a quagmire. Sometimes a lorry would meet another one coming in the opposite direction and then one of them would have to reverse until a gate could be found leading into a field to give a retreat to one party until the other had gone by. And it was not unusual for a van sent to a farm gradually to sink into the mud as it was loaded up; that meant a further wait until a caterpillar-tracked machine could be fetched to drag the lot free. The intricate maze of lanes became a nightmare to the drivers, so many of whom were strangers. Signposts had been removed all over the country now, in case of enemy infiltration, and as the people moved out and the houses became empty there was no one from whom anyone could ask the way. But the snag caused by two vans or cavalcades meeting in these lanes was quickly dealt with by the transport officer who set up a one-way traffic system.

Some of the big houses were full of the kind of possessions which required professional packing, so a well known removal firm was called in. But they had not sufficient transport to deal with so much in such a short time, and at their request yet more pantechnicons were commandeered. There were some who, hoping to help the lorry drivers, carried many of their possessions out of their houses as soon as they knew they were on the next day's list to move—in fact in some cases the farm lanes were so muddy that the drivers would be unwise to try to drive along them. That November was both cold and wet but often bales and bundles were carried out with the boxes and cases, left in the open, and got soaked through. One old man said he had to sleep on damp bedding until the summer sun came to dry it out for him! It also became quite a common sight to see bales of hay and straw at the junction of these sad little lanes, awaiting collection, though most farmers were careful not to put them out in the rain without a cover. Many ricks had to be dismantled and baled and tons of mangels and other roots were carted away; there was to be compensation paid for those roots left in the ground, but such waste of feeding stuffs was very worrying for some.

Although the co-operation was wonderful, there were, inevitably, one or two who could not understand—like the old man of over eighty who had lived all his life in the cottage in which he had been born. He lived right in the centre of one of the villages, he knew everybody and everybody knew him. He had never moved away anywhere; even World War I had not disturbed him for he had gone on working on the farm which employed him just as though nothing was happening. Rumour had it that there had been a girl in his life once, but before he could get the banns called some quicker thinking fellow from 'up country' had snatched the girl away from him and he had never looked at another one. So when a messenger from one of the Information Centres called to see if he could make any plans to help himself, he replied that he had heard of some outlandish tale about moving people away but that he 'didn't want no truck wi' it, thank 'ee.'

'But you must,' said the worried caller, 'You'd be here all by yourself; look, we'll find you a nice place to stay and we'll look after your furniture for you.' But the old man was not to be cajoled and finally the messenger went outside where she contacted a neighbour. 'He's a nice old boy but obstinate,' said this woman, who then went on to explain that the old man was suffering badly with rheumatism and simply did not understand what all this business was about—'He's lost touch with the world really.' The messenger hurried back to the Centre and the old man was put on the 'difficult' list. Arrangements were made for him in due course, with the help of the doctor, but when moving day came he watched the packing being done as if in a dream, then sat on a packing case outside the gate and still refused to budge. This was one of the cases which had to be dealt with by great tact and genuine sympathy, for such an upheaval was almost the end of the world for the old man.

In contrast, there was the case of someone who, living over a hundred miles away, visited the Area to try to ensure that her holiday home, used almost exclusively for summer lettings, should remain intact, furniture and all. It was explained that she was acting foolishly and that it was impossible to make exceptions, but it was only when it was pointed out that the house was so near the coastline that anything might happen to it that she gave way. Reluctantly she agreed to conform and the removal was begun.

Happily, there were lighter moments too. One elderly spinster came to the Centre asking for help to capture and crate her hens which she was proposing to take with her on the following day, by train, to her new home. She explained, a little apologetically, that some were 'tame' and easily dealt with, but that others were 'wild' and could only be captured unawares! So some long-suffering helper, armed with the inevitable dimmed-out torch, had to be on the spot at 5.30 on a black, cold December morning, to snatch the supposedly sleeping hens off their perches and pop them, one by one, into the travelling crate.

As evacuation progressed, the sadness which was creeping over the land was reflected in the cases of so many of the elderly. There were many heartbreaks. For instance, one old lady had lived next door to an old man all her life, both had married and had lost their partners, and they could not be found billets anywhere near each other. They had to leave in deep regret and it was hoped that they both would be able to go back to their homes once the emergency was over, but unhappily, one died before the return. Some knew instinctively that, once moved away, they would never return, like the elderly widow who, gazing sadly round her pretty little home, whispered as she fought back the tears, 'I know I shall never come back again.'

For some of the elderly people the idea of moving out was too much to bear. There was a man and his wife, for example, both over eighty, who fell ill on being told what was going to happen. It was only with the greatest difficulty that hospital beds were found for them and the ambulance arrived at a stated time to take them away. Some of the sting was taken out of their departure however as the old man suddenly remembered his life savings, and great excitement was caused as he sent one of the stretcher bearers up to his loft to collect a box. This was put on the stretcher by his side, but not before he had opened it and displayed a handsome collection of golden sovereigns and half-sovereigns. But, tragically, they both died within a fortnight, from shock and disturbance. There was another elderly woman who became so terribly upset that she had a heart attack and died on her own doorstep. A tragic case was that of an old man who became so overwrought that he attempted to commit suicide. The suggestion of having to leave had so preyed on his mind that he would not agree to any offer of alternative accommodation. His wife had found somewhere for them to go and was willing to make the arrangements but he would have none of it. He was rescued from death in the nick of time by a hastily summoned district nurse and a helpful passer-by but he died a week or so after his abortive attempt.

There is the story, however, of the lucky old man who escaped death by a matter of a few hours during the time when the Evacuation was taking place. He had been bedridden for some time and arrangements were being made for him to be taken to relations. Meanwhile, as his bedroom was on a first floor and the house in a rather exposed position, those around him had been trying to get him moved downstairs, but he flatly refused to budge. At last the doctor was so insistent that the old man gave way. He was taken down to the ground floor and that very evening a passing tip and run plane dropped a bomb which exploded nearby, casting splinters of shrapnel into the bedroom he had just vacated, shattering furniture and the actual bed he had just left.

A lighter moment concerned two old fishermen. All their stuff was to go into store, gear, boat, all their joint possessions, but they insisted upon one article of furniture going with them into their temporary home—their piano!

It was not only the elderly who were affected by the general clearout; it had a psychological effect upon some children, particularly on those who loved the sea and hated the idea of having to go far away from their playmates, their pets and their familiar haunts. Some of them, like many old people, had a premonition that for one reason or another they would never come back and, of course, there were one or two minor tragedies. There was one, for instance, which would sum up for ever the disturbance of the hurried move in the mind of one small boy. His family found somewhere to go for the temporary banishment and arrangements to move were made; the removal men arrived and soon the van was half filled. But in the hustle and bustle, as pieces of furniture, cases and so on were brought out and were standing along the garden path, the shake-up released the catch of the pet rabbit's hutch. The door gently swung open and Mr Rabbit, with two or three agile hops, was out of the garden and 'away to go' across the fields. The boy, when he saw what had happened, just froze with grief; he was discovered by his mother standing staring at the empty hutch, tense and tearless in his childhood tragedy. His mother did her best, but all the fun and excitement had gone out of the move for this one small boy.

Nor could all the animals in the Area be saved. The Royal Society for the Prevention of Cruelty to Animals had many an unhappy task in having, for one reason or another, to put down many well beloved family pets. Many cats and dogs were transported to new temporary homes but even so some of these, particularly the cats, made quite long journeys to come back to familiar surroundings. One such cat survived all the subsequent bombings and managed to remain near his old home until his mistress returned a year later. He rejoiced in the splendid name of Adolphus Tips. The Americans, when they arrived, quickly adopted any strays they came across, feeding and looking after them until they, too, had to leave. The RSPCA also had to deal with a request by one woman for something to be given to her several cats to put them to sleep for a longish train journey. The official had to explain to her that such temporary sleep was impossible and that what he could give would be for ever, a fact which she accepted with a certain amount of indignation. It would be interesting to know how the problem was finally solved.

Taking the evacuation as a whole, however, it was astonishing how quickly some families got away once the initial difficulties had been solved. The countryside began to look untidy; some farmers took away their gates with them, the churned up lanes presented an uncared for appearance, while untended private gardens became thoroughly weed-ridden. 'There was just that feeling of being on an island that has been evacuated', said one man afterwards. The neglected fields looked unfamiliar to those who knew the Area well, while the lanes indeed began to resemble ploughed fields as convoys of heavily laden lorries battled their way to and fro. And this gradually settling air of desolation was only the beginning of the inevitable neglect. However, bit by bit, the whole operation took shape until what had seemed at times almost an impossibility gradually began to be straightened out.

A local doctor said that one of his most tricky tasks was to get several bedridden elderly people into hospital, accommodation in which was at a premium at this stage of the war, but miraculously the patients were finally all found beds somewhere. There was a flu epidemic during the six weeks; in fact one of the vicars and his wife were both down with it when the removal men came to clear the vicarage; there were also two funerals. One day a woman scheduled to leave on a certain date came into one of the Centres to announce, 'My child has German measles, how can I leave?' The doctor found it necessary to administer sedatives in many cases, especially among the elderly and where there was much depression, and his words of advice and comfort were more important than ever. It was not until very near the end of the six weeks that he found somewhere to go himself, to a house in Kingsbridge which had received bomb damage and which was repaired just in time for him to transport his family and his surgery. His practice naturally was cut considerably as many of his patients disappeared, but those outside the Area could still be visited though it meant a considerable trek sometimes to get around the cordoned off district.

One of the village butchers living on the edge of the Area found, in much the same way, that about half his customers still remained, as they lived outside the boundary. So, with his family, he was given accommodation by relatives, a friend lent him part of a garage which was made into a lock-up shop, and he worked from the Portlemouth side of the Kingsbridge estuary. Unluckily there was no electricity at that time in this particular village, so his refrigerator couldn't be used; however a cousin in Salcombe lent him a part of his for the weekends. This meant ferrying across the water each time he wanted to use the refrigerator and, moreover, arranging the trip at high tide, to get as near as possible to the premises. 'About half the business was left,' he said, adding that 'half a loaf is better than none.'

The problem of feeding those who still remained in the Area became an urgent one and this was one of the cases where the splendid gift of so many Ford Ten vans made at the beginning of the war by Henry and Edsell Ford came in so usefully. They were constructed so that half of one side would let down if necessary, providing a counter from which meals, etc, could be dispensed. Many, in fact, were used to convey hot midday dinners to country schoolchildren in many other parts of the country, the meals being cooked in a central kitchen and delivered in insulated containers. Some of these vans were sent to the Area, for, as the shops and inns closed, it became necessary for emergency meals to be distributed. One van was painted on the outside:

Food Flying Squad
Presented by
The People of Singapore, Malaya.

Emergency kitchens in the Area were mostly set up in tents, and in view of the damp weather which lasted for almost the whole of the six weeks they were not very comfortable places in which to work. The Navy provided personnel to cope with the heavier jobs but for many of the WVS helpers, who were without exception quite untrained for working in such rough conditions, it became a little hard. Nevertheless the meals were prepared, placed in containers, loaded into vans and delivered to all who needed them, the list gradually lessening as the end of December drew near. One worker said that as she and her companion driver drove up to one house due to be vacated two days later, they were received with coolness and even ingratitude —they were quite self-sufficient, thank you, said the householder, who seemed almost offended at being offered a hot dinner. But that was an isolated case for most people were really glad to have food brought to them in this rapidly emptying neighbourhood. Their furniture, including all kitchen equipment, was being packed away, and many would have been in real difficulties to find food for the last day or two.

Most of the shops had closed by now too and they also provided a problem for the transport organisers, as not only had furniture and personal belongings to be removed, but the contents of the shops also had to be carried away, and any perishable stuff disposed of outside the Area as soon as possible.

As the people moved out, the villages, once so warm and friendly, became strangely quiet. A stray dog, appearing at the top of a usually busy street, stopped in his tracks and stared as if asking 'Where has everybody gone?' A broken window frame banged in the breeze with a mournful sound and a rat, seemingly aware that his enemy, the human being, had unaccountably disappeared, made a leisurely tour of passages and little gardens, seeking food in unaccustomed places. Meanwhile the voluntary workers cooked and served the emergency meals, staffed emergency clinics and nurseries, advised those needing help and assistance, helped clear houses, packed up belongings, and were ready at a moment's notice to undertake any task, however menial, in order to spur forward the tremendous trek.

The daily progress report at each of the Centres steadily became bigger. When a property was vacated the householder had to report that the move was complete, give answers to many questions which were noted down, then this document was duly signed, handed over to the Centre, together with the keys, and that householder was officially 'out'. This list was now signed by one of the officials and filed. There was an elderly widow who, with her son and daughter, worked a small farm, and who had hardly left her home for years. Even the son and daughter had scarcely been off the premises since their schooldays. The widow by now was such a recluse that she found it well-nigh impossible to make the trip to the nearest Centre to get advice and help and complete the final documents. But arrangements had to be made and in the end their departure was conducted satisfactorily and with grateful thanks on behalf of the family.

Besides the wellbeing of the people, the welfare of the six parish churches, all but one of which were pre-Reformation and had many treasures, caused much anxiety. Slapton, Blackawton, East Allington, Sherford and Stokenham each have ancient and beautiful buildings; the one at Strete being the only so-called modern one, having been built during the last century. Stokenham serves both Torcross and Chillington. The Admiralty informed the Ecclesiastical Commissioners that it was impossible to guarantee the safety of any of these churches so an ecclesiastical sculptor from Exeter was called in to suggest what could be done. With his foreman and an American commander he toured each church in turn and recommended that any portable treasures such as silver candlesticks, crosses, crucifixes, vestments and other items should be taken away altogether by the churchwardens and stored elsewhere. Valuable but immovable items such as pulpits, fonts, monuments and tombs, windows and doors, should be heavily sandbagged, and the work was to begin at once. There being nowhere for the men from Exeter to stay, either inside or just outside the Area, they had to make the nearly forty-mile journey each day in very uncomfortable conditions as it was mostly in the blackout. The actual protecting of the churches went smoothly enough, for the work waiting to be done was what the men were trained to do; there was no need for improvisation.

American help was promised but the first two churches were finished by the sculptor, his foreman and another workman working entirely alone before the men arrived. One of their biggest tasks was to ensure that a tremendous amount of old woodwork was safely packed in straw in wooden boxes. These very old carvings were mostly from the fifteenth-century chancel screens which are a feature of many Devon churches—'brittle as gingerbread some of them', as the foreman put it. Most had been attacked by woodworm, but they were all so beautiful and so well worth preserving that the utmost skilled attention was given to handling them. Organs, arches and much stonework had also to be sandbagged, boardings had to be erected where practical, and finally the whole property locked and secured with barbed wire.

American help came when the third church was under way and then a sergeant appeared; but seeing the delicacy of the carvings which at that moment were being taken off the top of a fifteenth-century screen, he said, 'I'm afraid my men would be of no use to you. They've been trained to do rougher work.' He placed a tentative forefinger near a piece of carving which he obviously regarded, quite rightly, as gossamer, and shook his head. So another sergeant came and his opening speech gave great delight. Chewing gum and striding purposefully down the centre aisle, he demanded, 'Where's Norman's font we hear so much about?' And, as an afterthought, 'Who was he, anyway?' But he stayed to help, for his men could make boxes for the carvings which were to be taken away and stored; only he was not too keen on the foreman explaining how one box was to be made. 'I can make a box without instruction,' he said, but the laugh was on the other side when it was discovered that his measurements had been so generous that it was only with the greatest difficulty and manoeuvring that the box could be eased out of the porch and through the lych gate. However, the sergeant and the foreman became good friends after this. All in all the American soldiers were very useful indeed in many different ways, for not only were they able to help carry the wooden boxes full of carvings but they took their jeeps to the beach and filled the necessary sandbags which they then piled four or five feet high round the pulpits, tombs, doors, windows and fonts in the churches. Over the centuries each ancient church must have seen many different types of procession, some happy, some solemn and sad, but never before had there been this strange procession of American soldiers each carrying a sack of sand down the church paths and aisles and for such a worthy cause.

On each church's principal gate was now fastened the following notice:

> To our Allies of the U.S.A.
>
> This church has stood here for several hundred years. Around it has grown a community, which has lived in these houses and tilled these fields ever since there was a church. This church, this churchyard in which their loved ones lie at rest, these homes, these fields are as dear to those who have left them as are the homes and graves and fields which you, our Allies, have left behind you. They hope to return one day, as you hope to return to yours, to find them waiting to welcome them home. They entrust them to your care meanwhile, and pray that God's blessing may rest upon us all.
>
> Charles,
> Bishop of Exeter.

In the Area there were also the chapels of various denominations, but without exception they were simple buildings not possessing any ancient structures of wood or stone requiring professional attention. All portable valuables were carried away and stored at the discretion of the ministers concerned.

During the last week or two of the Evacuation, sentries appeared and all tradesmen were forbidden to enter. The threshing was nearly complete, the sacks of corn were filled and delivered, some people paid flying visits to their homes to pick up things left behind in the rush, gardens were ransacked of winter sprouts and so on, but much kale, mangolds and turnips on the farms had to be left. The Land Army called for more assistance and Naval Reservists were drafted in to help, along with prisoners from Exeter jail and servicemen home on leave; also many farmers from just outside the Area came in to give a hand in spite of the extra work they had on their own land. One WVS member managed to get in almost at the last moment to collect big baskets of winter vegetables from deserted gardens, for one of the undertakings of these volunteers was to try to supply fresh vegetables to the crews of minesweeper vessels.

Some American officials, already installed in their headquarters at the Manor House, Dittisham, appeared in the early part of December, anxious lest the Exodus should not be finished in time. Empty desolation was everywhere and the few people still waiting to be moved had quite a shock if they saw anyone approaching. Most wives had left by now and were trying to organise their new homes, but many of the farmers stayed behind for another week or so, giving a hand in many ways, including feeding and looking after the Christmas poultry which could not be killed too early as there were very few refrigerators in the country in those days. There was one farmer and his wife who stayed almost until the last day to supply milk to the scattered people, and their home became a kind of meeting place at mealtimes for those men who had stayed behind to help in various ways. Apparently there were eighteen people to tea on the last day they were there. This particular farmer and his wife were also the first to return in their village once the restrictions were lifted, for their farmhouse was undamaged.

An official on a round of inspection just before the final date had several unexpected encounters in the cold darkness of evening. Every dwelling was checked as it became officially empty, and once while walking over what he supposed was a deserted farmyard he heard a menacing voice shout, 'Stop—or I'll send a shot o' lead up the seat of yer trousis—there b'aint no more vowles for 'ee tonight, you 'ad 'em all last night.' It appeared that the man was due to go away in the morning and during the previous night someone had stolen a quantity of his Christmas birds, so he was determined to watch over what remained even if he had to sit up all the night. The same official had a second shock on another occasion when, again in approaching darkness —or what is more properly described in Devon as 'the dimpsey' —he found a pair of shining eyes staring unwinkingly up at him in the feeble light of his dimmed torch; it took him a second or two to get over the surprise before he realised it was a dead sheep.

In the fields now there was no movement, no cattle, no contented cows slowly drifting down the village at milking time; farmyards were unnaturally still; there were no horses, no sheep or pigs, and over everything there crept an unreal, slightly fantastic air. The trimmest gardens quickly deteriorated, crops left in the ground struggled with the weeds. Up in the hills the matting strip laid down for aircraft landing looked odd in its setting. It was curious, too, to see a card stuck in the window of a cottage in one village—the official government card issued to all householders, all over the country, who took evacuated schoolchildren into their homes. These cards were intended to be put into the window, and nearly always were, but in this case it seemed to strike an ironic note, for those who had been willing to give shelter in the early war days had now been obliged to look for shelter for themselves.

One old man and his wife turned up at one of the Centres saying they had been living for the past three days in their home with one table, two chairs and a bed, eating cold meals and waiting for the butcher to collect their poultry. They were both amazingly cheerful about it, but when an official suggested they must have left in a hurry for the old man had not even laced his boots, he replied that the laces had been eaten by rats! The rats, naturally enough, increased tremendously during this and the following months, and already were becoming visible in numbers where before they had remained hidden.

A WVS organiser who owned a roomy car arranged to take the last family from one of the villages to Newton Abbot on the very last day. The family had on one pretext or another refused to go earlier, and even now the furniture had only been moved for storage that very morning. Of all the jobs the organiser had done throughout the six weeks she said this was one of the worst. She could not fetch them until six in the evening and by then it was pitch dark and there was an 'alert' on, which meant enemy aircraft somewhere near. The family had not even started to pack personal belongings but as the driver had taken a friend with her for company on the lonely way back, they did their best between them to get a little organisation into the proceedings.

There were clocks to go, a parrot in a cage, loose clothing, a couple of dilapidated suitcases, unfastened brown paper parcels, a kitten, a crying child and three adults; and when all was packed into the car there was not an inch to spare. The kitten got loose during the journey not once but three times and the driver said her elbows were rammed so hard into her sides that she could hardly change gear.

And what were the conditions under which such a night time drive in war had to take place? Headlights had to be hooded and sidelights subdued by tissue paper behind the glass; there were few white lines and no sparkling little studs every few yards in the centre of the country roads; no street lighting anywhere and no lights shining from the houses—an Air Raid Warden or Home Guard official would soon knock up a house where curtains were not properly drawn, even if only a tiny shaft of light showed. The only hope for a car to keep going was to drive as near the hedge as possible and to go slowly. There was, mercifully, very little traffic on the roads in any case. On this particular occasion, however, an enemy bomb was dropped on a village a few miles away resulting in a fire, all of which added to the tension.

This nightmare journey reached Newton Abbot in due course and a friendly policeman set them in the right direction for the lodgings which had been booked for the family. But it was with great thankfulness that the driver turned the car homewards—and as she did so the 'all clear' siren sounded.

A letter written by a WVS worker who was deeply concerned in the evacuation said that 156 WVS members were involved in the great task and that all other war work in which they were engaged had to take second place. The letter goes on:

> ... an epidemic of flu has added to the difficulties of finding personnel for the Information Bureaux, the semi-mobile kitchen, the Home Guard canteen, packing squads and drivers. This is a tremendous undertaking and helpers have come from far and near to help forward the Evacuation. One feels that these villages will be forever inscribed in our memory—the appalling muddy lanes made worse by an ever growing fleet of lorries and numerous Voluntary Car Pool cars. The pathetic sight of the old and infirm at the Bureaux, all seeking advice, the R.S.P.C.A. vans, disposing of pets that cannot be taken away, are all heart-rending. The only consolation is that were the enemy invading all personal belongings would have to be left behind.

Volunteers were sent at the last to inspect every village, to make sure that everyone had gone, that each house or cottage was properly secured and that all was in readiness to be officially handed over to the American authorities. One WVS helper sent to check a coastal village found that on this particular morning the sun was shining brightly, the blue sea was calm and sparkling, gulls were flying happily overhead as she walked, conscientiously, round every dwelling, checking as she went. But in spite of the lovely crisp morning there was something unreal and creepy about it. She looked in all the windows and tried all the doors and not a soul was in sight. 'It was very sad and eerie', she said. 'Just one black cat walked across the road—that was the only sign of life there was in the whole village.'

The stage was set.

FOUR
Occupation

THERE MUST BE PEOPLE IN THE TOWN OF SALCOMBE, just outside the Area, who can remember, as children, being invited to a Christmas party on board an American Red Cross ship moored in the estuary. The crew, who had voted to provide this, acted as waiters at a splendid tea and Father Christmas, carrying a sack of candy—the men's own rations—dispensed very welcome 'off the ration' goodies. The crew and the children played games together and finally each child, and there were 150 Salcombe schoolchildren, was given a present on leaving. It was a much-appreciated gesture. But there was not a single lighted tree, not a decoration nor one visit from Father Christmas in the Area; all was hushed and waiting. Actually it was not entirely empty for there was the small advance group of US troops who had already arrived and had immediately posted sentries.

On the two or three days before Christmas, American troops arrived in the Area in great numbers. The liners *Queen Mary* and *Queen Elizabeth* had been bringing US troops across the

Atlantic for some time. Shorn of all unnecessary trimmings each ship could carry 15,000 men on each trip, and when those men scheduled for the Area arrived in the South Hams a cordon was drawn around and all was silent. But the silence was soon to be broken by the sound of battle as the exercises began and red flags were run up at special points if live ammunition was being used, to warn those living near.

Sometimes great activity was seen in Start Bay; ships would appear from where they were moored in estuaries and other sheltered spots up and down the coast, but local people were not able to see much owing to the 'Out of Bounds' notices and the lie of the land. The one local individual who really could see what was going on was a Coast Watcher whose beat took him into places forbidden to the general public. A Naval Reserve man, he had been called up in 1941 to patrol a certain part of the coast and even now, two years later, there were only six of them to watch, day and night, six hours on and six hours off, a very long stretch of the cliffs. This particular man's beat took him right up to the border of the Area and he met and talked with many of the sentries 'over the fence' as it were. He also reported many casualties on the beach as time went on and the exercises became more and more realistic. The beauty and peace had gone. Sometimes, he said, the bay would be quite empty and still, and in a few hours it would be absolutely full of ships of all descriptions and sizes, including landing craft and DUKWs. The latter were amphibious wheeled trucks which could carry twenty men, motor as a boat from a ship and then drive up the beach. There is no doubt that the training was punishingly severe and there were times when the men could be seen to be utterly exhausted with the stresses and strains put upon them, as they occasionally came ashore in small parties on the beaches just outside the Area. On the other hand, they would have a few hours' leave at times when, smartly attired, they would make their way to Dartmouth or Kingsbridge where they quickly made friends.

January and February went by and it was beginning to be realised by local people that some sort of confrontation with Hitler's men would take place in the coming summer and, although the occupation of the Area was now on such a massive scale, it is almost unbelievable how little of the scheme was known to the general public outside the South Hams itself. All concerned were warned not to talk about it, for as one poster frequently seen in public places declared, 'Careless Talk costs Lives'.

The Coast Watcher had several interesting encounters while patrolling on duty during the Occupation. One day he heard men talking just over the hedge in an out-of-bounds part; he leapt over the hedge to confront two uniformed men who immediately challenged him at the same moment that he challenged them. He was a little taken aback as he realised that he was talking to General Eisenhower and General Montgomery who were waiting for an exercise to begin. They complimented him on his strict attention to duty but 'Monty' told him to go no further along his path as shelling was about to start at any moment; should he be reprimanded for not continuing his beat, he was to mention his, Monty's, name. On another occasion he met a party of three or four people close to the Area's boundary, including Princess Marie-Louise. She was most interested in his work, asking questions about the conditions, and the next week she sent a parcel of warm clothing to him and his colleagues, for they were not issued with uniform. The parcel consisted of Balaclava helmets, British warms, gloves, scarves and so on. Ultimately she gave a tea party for his little group, as she was living in Devon at the time.

Meanwhile damage was being suffered in the Area itself from the shelling and bombing. The well known Royal Sands Hotel, halfway along Slapton Sands, already partly destroyed before the troops arrived, was blown sky-high on one occasion, never to be rebuilt. Another time a former guest house, high up on the hill at Torcross, was hit by a misdirected bomb; it was being used as an officers' headquarters and reports had it that many officers were killed in the explosion. The building had been commandeered by the Navy in 1940, presumably as a possible headquarters should one be necessary as time went on. On another occasion a shell exploded in the Ley, killing many fish which were blown right out of the water. As it was now the nesting season all bird life was destroyed, including the water-line birds which were down on their nests. It was a couple of years or so before songs and chirpings were heard in the Area again, and several years more before some of the less frequent varieties of migrants came back to the neighbourhood.

During the occupation the local Home Guard was asked by Western Command to provide a group to undertake night patrols round the outside of the Area during the hours of 2.30 am to 4.30 am. This mobile company was raised from younger men in the local Home Guard battalion, mostly farmhands, who had already done a good day's hard work. They were issued with modern weapons and cars, and the Women's Voluntary Service supplied a mobile canteen. At first they were looked upon rather as a joke by the practising troops but, one night, during a test in which troops were landed on Slapton Sands and had proceeded to march in the direction of Kingsbridge, the patrol spotted the soldiers. The Home Guard battalion was alerted and within forty minutes had 'dug in' at Frogmore Bridge. The decision of the umpire was that the Home Guard had wiped out the invaders, his main point being that he considered it astonishing for them to have arrived so quickly on the spot. After this test the Home Guard was accorded a certain respect although the major in charge of the mobile group stated that one of their chief troubles was lack of information as to the previous day's fighting; shell holes in the boundary roads were frequently not reported so that on dark nights their cars sometimes would end up in craters.

On one occasion during an exercise a German submarine surfaced in Start Bay, right in the midst of many ships of all kinds and sizes, and it is to be feared that many lives were lost on both sides. It was driven off ultimately but for some time afterwards reprisals were expected, as surely the enemy must have realised that here was an immense accumulation of men and war material which would have been a wonderful target for the Luftwaffe. But the Nazi planes had taken a severe knocking by now and their sorties were becoming fewer. It might be possible also, that the submarine never got back to base to report its findings.

As already mentioned there were, regrettably, casualties on the beaches from time to time but the worst experience was an engagement with the enemy at sea in April, during one of the full-scale rehearsals, when nine German E-boats from Cherbourg who were prowling about at midnight managed to elude the watching patrols in Lyme Bay and attack some of the rehearsing ships. One of the latter was torpedoed and, although the resulting gun flashes warned five of her companions which had not yet bombarded Slapton Sands—after which their troops would have landed unless repulsed—the torpedoed ship burst into flames and finally the survivors had to abandon ship. For about half-an-hour shots were exchanged between the E-boats and the landing boats, together with two British destroyers which were in the covering force, but the enemy escaped by the use of smoke and speed. It is reported that the loss of life in this one action was greater than that of the US troops on Utah beach in Normandy on D Day.

So the exercises went on and spring came to Devon. A few

hardy souls living just outside the Area and who knew the lie of the land well had no difficulty whatever in creeping into the Area to see how things were shaping, as long as the red flags were not flying. Of course it meant running the risk of being discovered by the Americans but, as far as is known, this rarely happened. One man went in regularly to snare rabbits. Having made sure that everything was clear for the moment he would make for a deep ditch in which to hide if necessary, or an old linney behind which he could stand unseen. Finally, when all seemed safe, he would arrange his snares in a rabbit run. He could easily find a ready market for a nice fresh rabbit as the meat ration was by then very scanty, and that's the way he earned his beer money. He was not the only one who did this either, though it was never safe to go far away from the boundary. But, on the whole, such encroachments were not a very frequent occurrence as the hazard of unexploded ammunition was too great and rarely, if ever, did an illegal visitor penetrate far inside the Area.

One farmer and his wife who had decided to risk an entry into the Area to visit their farm during the Occupation were actually invited in by some troops. The man was young enough to have been called up into one of the services and so it was during a short leave that they decided upon the great adventure. There were no red flags flying and their home was near the border so, as the wife was spending the Evacuation with her parents not very far away, they were able to walk to one of the more secluded parts of the Area and proceed down a rather rutted lane. They soon discovered why the lane was so very used looking as almost immediately a US jeep came roaring up the hill with four coloured soldiers aboard. Leaping for the hedge, the farmer and his wife smiled a little tentatively at the soldiers, not knowing in quite what manner their illegal appearance would be taken; but when they explained that the object of their visit was just to see their home and its surroundings, the men were all benevolent smiles and all four answered at once, 'Sure, you can come right in. Yes, sar, go straight on down' and other encouraging remarks. So the young farmer and his wife walked gaily on, amused to think that they were being politely invited to look at their own property. Incidentally they found it in good repair, dirty and forlorn-looking but as sound as when they had left it—the only present occupants were pigeons, who seemed in complete possession of the farmhouse garden; which was curious as all other bird life had either flown out of the Area or had been killed. But no doubt they were visitors from outside.

Another incident concerned the doctor, who was on his way round the Area to visit a patient on the other side when he passed his own home which could be seen from the boundary road. Glancing across to it he saw that the kitchen chimney was smoking. Now he knew that the main water had been turned off and that if the tank of hot water was emptied an explosion might, in fact was almost certain, to follow. So throwing caution to the winds, he left his car, crept down the lane and entered the forbidden territory to warn the soldiers in the house of their danger. As he had taken no pains to hide as the rabbit catcher did, this was one of the few illegal entries which was found out. A visit from the police followed and the doctor was fined. But it was a small price to pay, he felt, for averting what might have been a real tragedy.

Actually the plan had been that every house, cottage and farm should be locked and the keys were handed over to the authorities at the time of the Evacuation. But keys or no keys, practically every door was opened by some means during the exercises and no doubt the empty houses afforded shelter to the troops during the spring of 1944. However, as will be seen later, many unauthorised people gained access to the Area after the troops had left, making it impossible to blame the soldiers for everything that went awry. In fact, there were instances of premises where no damage from ammunition had occurred being still in excellent order when the troops left, but during the time that the Area was still closed officially to the general public, the thieving and wanton destruction was almost unbelievable. The dishonest invaders assumed that the blame would lie firmly on the backs of the troops who, having departed to the battleground in France, could hardly be called upon to put the facts right. This is not to say that soldiers had not entered houses, but a great deal of the thieving, petty destruction and other damage was proved to be the work of unscrupulous sneak thieves. American servicemen had been in this country for a long time before the training ground in the South Hams was lent to them and their reputation for good behaviour was generally of the highest.

Soon after the US entry into the war, a big American hospital was built on nine holes of an eighteen-hole golf course not far from Newton Abbot, where wounded or sick could be treated in the comparative solitude of the countryside. After the war this camp was reorganised, and when the hospital moved out it was handed over to the many Polish refugees who had arrived by a most circuitous route after being promised safety and a home by Winston Churchill. It still exists today, pleasantly laid out and occupied chiefly by the elderly as the younger generation has by now been largely absorbed into local life.

As for the thousands of US troops awaiting for the invasion in 1944, apart from those who just set up camps in every available space in South Devon, sleeping in tents or trucks and giving the impression that the entire American army was parked there, in some cases a few were squeezed into private houses. One such group was found billets in a Devon watering town in a big Victorian house overlooking the sea. The house was occupied by a professional man engaged in an important medical appointment, his wife and baby son, and also included that rarity of all rarities in wartime, a factotum to help while father and mother got on with their wartime activities. The property consisted of no fewer than eight bedrooms, three bathrooms and extensive basements. The billeting officer's eyes lit up with thankfulness at this information and he arranged that sixteen US troops should take possession in March 1943. Because of security reasons no particular date was given and the troops arrived at about 2 am one morning, having landed in Avonmouth after a particularly bad crossing, been brought down by lorry and then having spent a good hour or more chasing round the town looking for their billet. They were ushered into the drawing-room where they spent the rest of the night and most of the following morning asleep on the floor, their firearms neatly stacked on the Chippendale chairs. The GIs were a mixed bunch of varied racial extraction but seemed to mingle well as a group. One room was used by them as their laundry and, under the expert eye of the woman helper in the house, they quickly became so expert at washing and ironing that when they left they could all qualify as experienced laundrymen!

One of them worked in their local mess and canteen, and on one occasion he went to the owner of the house saying, 'Say, mister, would you like some frankfurters for your dawgs?'—there being two dogs in the household at the time, one as an evacuee. So an enormous carton of about 10lb of sausages was brought in that evening and sausage and mash was greatly enjoyed by all for a day or two afterwards, including of course a share for the canine friends. There was never any trouble with noise or drunkenness, and the householders said they had the happiest memories of their stay until just before D Day and were really sorry to see the soldiers go. Many of the men kept in touch for some years after the war, sending letters and cards at Christmas. It would seem that, like those many hundreds of others just waiting for the call to battle, these men were not front-line troops but men who were trained to do all kinds of different jobs necessary to back up the invasion once it had started. Periodically, in 1944, various groups of them were drafted into the Area to accustom the men to working under live ammunition; but it was a very harrowing experience for some to go from the comparatively sane and ordinary life of 'behind the lines' into the practice area, even if only for a short time. Indeed, their experience sometimes even reflected upon those with whom they were billeted. One such hostess said that one or two men were so obviously exhausted on their return from one such exercise that she herself began to feel the strain. For although the firing was always overhead it was a shattering experience, especially as few of the men were professional long-term servicemen.

In another case a smaller batch of men was placed in a largish house which had a big attic in which to accommodate them. There was a dignified dog here too, and true to their reputation of making friends easily with the local animals, the GIs soon made the dog almost one of themselves. He discovered that the men went to breakfast at a nearby church room which had been requisitioned as the cook-house, so he followed his housemates for nearly a week as they marched to their mess. He then decided that he had learned the drill, so after that he walked at the head of the column instead of following and he expected, and of course got, his share of breakfast too. He missed the men sadly when they left, just before the invasion. The lady of the house missed them also, for in common with so many people at that time of food shortages, she kept some hens in the garden and each evening she was presented with a parcel of 'plate scrapings' to augment the hens' diet. It was reported that the hens had never done so well and that they fully repaid this

Page 85 (above) *Evacuation completed—the empty main street of Chillington;* (below) *US soldiers move in, unloading truckloads of bunks*

Page 86 (above) *Two American soldiers assemble their machine-gun in their new quarters;* (below) *American soldiers and British sailors working together to unload a vehicle during invasion manoeuvres; the wire matting prevented vehicles sinking in the sand*

attention by producing really first-class eggs.

But wherever they went or were stationed, GIs made friends with the local people and many were the 'grin and pass on' friendships between them and some of the volunteer van-drivers who regularly passed them on wartime work such as delivering hot dinners to schools or other Women's Voluntary Service or Red Cross activities. One not very young driver was pulled up on one occasion when driving down a heath lined on both sides with camps, and requested with a grin to 'Just slow down to seventy miles an hour, will you?'

No one anywhere at this time could drive a civilian car of any sort without having been granted a permit to be on the road, and during the last few weeks before D Day it meant another permit still if there was any necessity to be on one of the roads leading to the south coast for however short a period. The mere crossing of one of these main roads to get from one side road or lane to another could be quite hazardous, even if it only meant having to traverse the main road for a matter of a few hundred yards, as a convoy rounding a bend and travelling at top speed could appear at any moment. Most of the main roads leading to the harbours were 'one way only' by now. One voluntary helper, just outside the Area and belonging to what was known as the 'dust group', which meant doing a real dustman's job in collecting the rubbish from a couple of villages, came round a corner one day and was confronted by signs saying 'Danger' and 'Five miles an hour', and there, piled up many feet high, were quantities of huge ammunition boxes all along the grass verge. But what really shook her was the appearance of a little coloured soldier sitting, happily smiling, right on the top—smoking!

There were, of course, enormous processions of war vehicles as early summer drew near. These gradually piled up near the harbours, most of their equipment being incomprehensible to

F

the normal civilian; it was just 'war stuff'. One day one of these big collections of mixed vehicles was approaching the Area by a rather narrow country lane, and there it was brought to a standstill by the appearance of a small private car, coming from the opposite direction and driven by a lady who had a tiny allowance for a once-a-week shopping trip as she lived in a remote spot. They all pulled up. The driver in the front vehicle called out to her to reverse to the nearest gateway and thus allow the army to pass. Either she was offended at being shouted at, or, what is more likely, she was unable to reverse (it was astonishing how many women in those days who only drove occasionally could not reverse) and she foolishly became haughty and refused to budge. This was quite absurd for there were nearly a dozen of these enormous American machines and had she but tried a little womanly charm no doubt one of the soldiers would have cheerfully done the job for her. But no, she sat in aloof silence and without more ado the cavalcade made up its mind. To the Americans' advantage the front vehicle was a crane, and quickly fastening chains round the little car, with the lady still inside, the latter was lifted bodily over the hedge into a field and left there while the soldiers proceeded on their way. A man working at the other end of the field heard the rumpus and put it down, rightly, to 'they Americans', but his amazement when he saw the little car coming over the hedge was unbelievable. However, he came to the lady's aid and finally got her out, this time by the gate. This tale was related by a man who had actually witnessed the whole drama.

Preparations for the invasion were now going rapidly ahead. English ports had never held so many ships and sailors, or the land so many troops, and although everywhere in the south was so very crowded, it was nevertheless an assurance to the British people that the long awaited invasion was at last to take place. Throughout May the huge convoys continued to roar along on the way to discreet parking grounds near the south-coast harbours, the faces of the men beaming with smiles as though to say, 'Look out, we're on our way to France!' It was action at last after months of waiting. Rivers and bays were now full of ships waiting to fill up with troops and war equipment to cross the Channel. In the River Exe, for instance, there were among other craft three or four ships bearing huge labels proclaiming that they were supply vessels, the labels reading 'Spares', 'Oil', 'Petrol', and so on; it seemed incredible that the enemy made no effort at all to bomb these sitting targets.

At the beginning of June the weather was poor and quickly deteriorated into heavy storms. The ships to convey land forces, their supplies and many types of vehicles were packed and ready but had to stand by for a week 'sealed in' as it were, awaiting instructions. General Eisenhower conducted the invasion operation for a few days from a train placed on the permanent way at Droxford, Hampshire, where he lived and worked during the crucial first day or two of the invasion, keeping in close touch with Air Marshal Tedder, General Montgomery, Field Marshal Smuts, General de Gaulle and Mr Winston Churchill. D Day was originally fixed for 5 June but such a severe gale blew up in the Channel that it was necessary to postpone operations for twenty-four hours. The invasion had to be either on the 6th or 7th or the whole plan would have had to be postponed for a fortnight, as the tides in Normandy would not be suitable for landings. Thousands of officers, therefore, had to be re-alerted, a not inconsiderable task in itself. In one Devon river, for instance, the chief pilot and his motor boat were commandeered and, with a naval officer aboard, they had to visit every one of the many ships riding at anchor and inform them of the change of plans.

Not many people could see the actual start of the invasion from the Area but one who did was the Coast Watcher. He was on duty on the usual cliff top when, at 1 am on 6 June the first planes went over. The storm had only abated a little but by 2 am the sky over Normandy was lit up like day by flares and search-lights. The vibrations of the allied ships blazing away at the coastal defences could be felt even on the cliff in Devon although it was roughly ninety miles away. Several villages near the coast also felt this heavy vibration.

Bit by bit at the appointed hour the jigsaw pieces of the huge invasion scheme began to fall into place. First the Channel had to be swept clear of submarines and mines, then the Allied planes flew over to hammer the shore batteries and radio installations in Normandy before the troops and vessels containing huge quantities of equipment crossed the Channel under an 'umbrella' of aircraft. There were more than 4,000 ships engaged, plus many smaller boats, including landing craft and DUKWs and the ships towing the Mulberry Harbours. Unfortunately the bad weather of 6 June was a mere prelude to the worst storm for forty years which happened on the 19th and this so damaged Mulberry 'A' that it was impossible to salvage it. It was the one allotted to the Americans but as the US 7th Corps under the command of Major General Joseph Lawton Collins had succeeded in capturing Cherbourg with its good harbour, the loss was not so great; not only did they capture the harbour but they took 20,000 German prisoners as well. Mulberry 'B', although damaged, was repaired from the ruins of 'A' and was set up as planned. When in full working order it was able to handle as much as 9,000 tons of supplies in a day, three times as much as expected.

As dawn broke on D Day, the fires started by the heavy bombers acted as beacons for incoming ships and there seemed an almost complete absence of the Luftwaffe. The tide was low, exposing many of the enemy's anti-invasion obstacles to view, but the little craft of the assault troops dodged these to run ashore; the men then darted up the sands in the face of rifle and machine-gun fire, for there were many concrete pill-boxes half underground and even the shelters for the sentries were reinforced holes in the ground with heavy concrete lids to pull over them. Troops and supplies were arriving on the beaches now in a steady flow with DUKWs going to and fro in an endless procession from the ships in the bay.

Now all the practice that those training grounds in Britain had provided for six months was being put into action. Some of the beach groups had actually landed on the Normandy coast even before the assault parties, and so were able to call the various craft into the beaches in correctly organised order—men and vehicles, supplies and stores, field dressing stations and so on—also to re-embark the wounded, and later to send prisoners of war to Britain. The appalling weather had probably helped to encourage the enemy into thinking that no great invasion scheme would be attempted until the storms died down. For the huge seas, raging high winds and heavy clouds all combined to make the plan a complete surprise to the enemy. The only part of the Normandy coast in any way especially protected was an area which was being used for anti-invasion exercises, a coincidence that caused heavy casualties. Altogether it was the biggest military operation the world had ever seen, the greatest Armada and involving the greatest accumulation of scientific know-how and equipment ever to come together in a fight for freedom.

Meanwhile, back in England, the Area now lay hushed and still. It remained out of bounds on account of the unexploded ammunition and the sentries were still there to keep people out. The land was shabby and uncared for, wounded in the same way that so many gallant men had been; but its people had given of their best and there is no doubt that the sacrifices of the evacuated people had been the means of saving many lives in the invasion of Normandy. On 7 June the joyous shouts of the people in Bayeux, the ancient Normandy town which was the first to be retaken, most fortunately undamaged, were so great and so heartfelt that they could almost have been heard in that curiously bereft part of Devon.

A few hours after the invasion had begun the Prime Minister told the House of Commons that:

> ...Reports are coming in in rapid succession. So far the commanders engaged report that everything is proceeding according to plan.
>
> And what a plan! This vast operation is undoubtedly the most complicated and difficult that has ever occurred. It involves tides, winds, waves, visibility, both from the air and the sea standpoint, and the combined employment of land, air and sea forces in the highest degree of intimacy and in contact with conditions which could not and cannot be fully foreseen. There are already hopes that actual tactical surprise has been attained, and we hope to furnish the enemy with a succession of surprises during the course of the fighting.
>
> The battle that has now begun will grow constantly in scale and in intensity for many weeks to come, and I shall not attempt to speculate upon its course. This I may say however. Complete unity prevails throughout the Allied Armies. There is a brotherhood in arms between us and our friends of the United States. There is complete confidence in the Supreme Commander, General Eisenhower, and his lieutenants, and also in the commander of the Expeditionary Force, General Montgomery. The ardour and spirit of the troops, as I saw myself, embarking in these last few days was splendid to witness. Nothing that equipment, science and forethought could do has been neglected, and the whole process of opening this great new front will be pursued with the utmost resolution both by the commanders and by the United States and British governments whom they serve.

Later in the day, Mr Churchill, who had promised to keep the House informed, made the following statement:

> I have been at the centres where the latest information is received and I can state that this operation is proceeding in a thoroughly satisfactory manner.

Meanwhile in Philadelphia, the historic Liberty Bell which heralded American Independence and bears the inscription 'Proclaim liberty throughout the land to all the inhabitants thereof', was tolled six times and broadcast throughout the country.

FIVE
The Gradual Return

ALMOST TOTAL SILENCE NOW DESCENDED UPON THE Area, in complete contrast to the violent and abrupt noises of the past six months. No movement, no cattle, no sign of life in the farms and villages, not even birds with cheerful songs were there bringing in the dawn, to break this curious feeling of emptiness; though actually a little human life was soon drafted in to assess the state of the land, and to make immediate plans to get things restored as soon as possible. Also US sentries were still on guard to keep out everyone who did not have a permit to enter, for there was an unknown quantity of unexploded ammunition about.

It is perhaps not quite accurate to say that there was no life at all, for in certain parts there were vast numbers of rats. Rabbits were abundant too, for both creatures were able to shelter underground when the shelling began. And curiously enough, although bird life was practically non-existent there were scores of pigeons in certain parts, as the young farmer and his wife had discovered when they visited their home during the

Occupation; these pigeons had probably bred outside the Area and, when the shelling had ceased, ventured into the silence to ravage where they wished. Also the cats and dogs, including quite a few sheep-dogs, which had returned to their old haunts (often walking many miles from their new homes) and had been befriended by the Americans were then left, perforce, in this curious silence, without companionship, shelter or food—the rabbits and rats came in handy in the latter instance.

By and large, however, the Area seemed to lie as if under a spell, beautiful still but neglected and forlorn, waiting for the touch of a magic wand to revive its normal life. But nature is never still, especially in the summer, and gradually the flowers and ferns helped to hide the ravages of war. Brambles covered the broken hedges, honeysuckle grew over the thistles, docks and much other vegetation struggled for space with wild hops, ivy and meadowsweet, but the great gashes made by the shells, the leafless trees, the broken banks—those could not be covered up in a hurry. This was man's ugly handiwork and must be put right by man, unless he was prepared to wait for a generation or two and even then it would only be uncultivated and wild beauty; his own hard work was necessary to achieve ordered success in cultivated country. In spite of the spell, there was also promise in that fertile ground as the dog roses and then good, rich blackberries tried to hide the disfiguring gaps. Though the blue sea still shimmered at the base of the hills, there was a sinister touch inland in this strange neglect of the acres which had been so carefully tended for centuries; and over all was this heavy, brooding silence, no drone of insects, no birdsong, no butterflies in the still air. When the winds blew it felt uncanny and the rains seemed to bring sadness, all adding to the devastation of battle.

Shell holes were plentiful in fields, roads, even gardens, especially in those near the coast. The South Hams is blessed with many beautiful trees and these suffered badly in many cases. They stood lifting leafless branches up to the sky but it was soon discovered that many others, though not actually killed, had lost their shape and design and even today a few of these can quite easily be picked out from those which were more or less untouched. The long, winding road leading uphill from Slapton sands to the village of Strete is bounded on each side by old stone walls which were hit in so many places that a child, on her return, told her mother that it looked as if a giant had taken big bites out of them!

However, when the last American truck had departed from the Area with all the equipment not needed for D Day, the ground was formally handed back to the Government. Rehabilitation of the land was in the hands of the War Agricultural Executive Committee, and the task of restoration started. First of all a bomb-disposal unit was sent in with mine detectors to seek out unexploded ammunition, and set to work in three stages: the outer perimeter first, then the centre, leaving the coastline, obviously the worst hit, until the last. The main object at first was to get back as many farmers as possible in time to make sure that at least a little autumn sowing could be done. Some farms naturally had been more hit about than others and the longer it took to repair the farmhouse the worse was the neglect on the land. A great deal also depended upon restoration of the roads. For farming could not really begin to get under way until the roads were repaired, especially in central and coastal places; they had to be safe for farm equipment, cattle and supplies. The rural-council men were sent in to repair the more important ones as soon as possible as enormous craters had to be filled in and then the damaged walls repaired; fences which had been literally torn to pieces by the passing of huge war equipment had to be sorted out to render the lanes passable. In some parts the little lanes had proved too narrow for some of the huge American vehicles so the troops had either flattened the hedges and banks or, more commonly, had filled the lanes with great loads of earth which raised their level to the bank tops. These alterations were not extensive but gave rise to great astonishment when the people returned. When vans were able to use the roads, main drainage, water, electricity and the telephone were restored by the appropriate companies. These modern amenities were by no means universal, especially in the more remote districts but, little by little, they gradually came to most places to the delight and comfort of the local inhabitants.

As soon as the mine detectors had been over the outer perimeter they moved systematically through the centre down towards the coast; following them came the surveyors and photographers with their previous records to assess the damage. Theirs was a long assignment and in some cases they were still at work two years afterwards. At the same time an absolute army of workers was drafted in—road repairers, engineers and builders, also those groups who had helped to move out the farmers, reinforced again by prisoners from Exeter jail (a welcome change for them) and Italian prisoners of war, who occupied a rough camp left by the troops. The complaint about the latter was that they were forever disappearing to trap rabbits—perhaps to vary camp catering! Officials from Seale Hayne Agricultural College came to give professional advice; an attempt was made to save a field of yarrow but that proved impossible, though they were able to gather a little late hay. Many of the crops left in the ground, kale, root vegetables and the like, proved quite a task as they were now sprouting and competing with the weeds; nevertheless one or two farms were, in spite of the difficulties, back in occupation again by the autumn. The agricultural botanist, Frank Horne, from Seale Hayne, whose advice had been so valuable in the days of the

Exodus, came again to advise on rehabilitation. Under his guidance the opportunity was later taken to test some new spring-sown wheat and in 1945 the value of the new Swedish 'Fylgia' and 'Atle' was demonstrated. There was much reseeding of grass during that autumn and as the farmers gradually returned they seemed to have renewed interest in their work, ready to try out fresh ideas, fresh methods.

The sentries had quite a difficult time at first keeping out anxious householders, for no permits for viewing properties were issued until mid-August. But to those who knew the country and who enjoyed a kind of sentry-dodging game there were several clandestine entries. For a while the sentries patrolling the Area were Americans left behind for the purpose; so on the off-chance that a coloured US soldier might not have enough knowledge of English voluntary bodies to guess he had no real responsibility, one man donned his Home Guard uniform, with his best authoritative manner, and waving his papers under the nose of a non-comprehending sentry, managed to enter and inspect his own house quite openly. It had been entered, as practically all properties had been, but was not in too bad a shape and he strode majestically out again, pleased that his little plan had succeeded.

On another occasion, a girl who had travelled back a good thirty miles to Kingsbridge market with her father, sometime in early July, thought that being so near the Area was too good an opportunity to miss; so, taking the family car and accompanied by a friend, she drove to a spot outside the Area but not too far from her home. Leaving her friend in the car as a wise precaution, she then proceeded to hide in the nearby woods. It was well known that a sentry passed by every twenty minutes or so and, biding her time, she then crawled along a deep dry ditch and was able to gain the shelter of the wall-enclosed farmyard. Here again, the doors were open and, creeping in quietly, she found the empty farmhouse more or less as they had left it, including an old chair they had thought too shabby to take. But what interested her most was the fact that every room was fitted with telephone wires—it must have been used as the telephone exchange by the occupying troops. Next, she visited the walled garden where she found quantities of raspberries and blackcurrants; the latter would have taken too long to pick individually so she broke off great clusters; then, picking a big bunch of flowers 'to take back to Mother', she departed the way she had come, unseen, unreported. 'Very quiet it was', she said, 'very, very dead quiet'. Soft fruit was particularly plentiful that year and the troops had gone away too soon to take advantage of it.

Incidentally a tremendous piece of good luck came to one of the Home Guard officers, who, quite officially, was taking a short cut through the large garden of a big house when he came upon a lemon tree. Citrus fruits were a thing of the past and bananas, when obtainable, were only issued on children's ration books, two or three at a time, but, owing to the benign climate of the South Hams and the sheltered position of the tree, there were real ripe lemons here just waiting to be picked. In such favoured spots quite a variety of unusual fruits will flourish, given a warm summer.

One day later that month a man and his schoolboy son crept back to their home by way of the ciffs for, actually, if the urge was strong enough and the fear of hidden shells weak enough, secret visits were apt to occur almost anywhere just inside the triangle which formed the Area. Without meeting anyone these two managed to reach home and slip inside. Again no keys were necessary. As they walked around they were glad to see the house was in good condition, but the yard outside surprised them considerably for the several barns and outhouses had all been removed so as to make a car park for the heavy vehicles which the troops had obviously wanted to store in this slightly sheltered spot. Father and son were so staggered by this unexpected sight that for a second they hardly knew where they were. Right in the middle of this emptiness was a small wooden post supporting a water tap—which had been inside a barn when they had seen it last! However, they were able to take back a glowing report of the house and, as for the condition of the yard, they knew that could be easily restored under the guarantee of full compensation for all such damage. All in all the father was very pleased with the condition of things as he had found them, fearing that the house could have been bombed, burnt down, or even totally destroyed.

He and his son took back a reassuring account and then, in October, he was given his permit to enter the Area officially. This time his wife came with him and they were both thunderstruck when they entered the house. In fact, had not their son been on the unofficial trip the wife would not have believed her husband's earlier report. One window had been smashed then—this time hardly a pane of glass remained in the entire house. They knew that the doors had been opened but now not a single brass door-handle was left; there was no brass knocker, none of the old-fashioned pull bells, in fact no brass fittings anywhere. (It must be remembered that absolutely nothing of this kind could be found in the shops any more—perhaps a second-hand shop might produce an odd piece or two but the price of such everyday articles would be out of all proportion to their real value.) Three doors had been removed bodily, an oak pedestal which they used as a support for their clock had disappeared and the brass container which held a lamp at the foot of the stairs had been ripped out. The wife was heartbroken at the thefts. 'I only wish I knew then as much as I do now,' said the man sadly, 'I could have dropped on the thieves, for I wasn't the only one to have a house ransacked; and it was nothing to do with the soldiers, they had left long before this happened—they'd gone before I paid my first visit.'

But that was a minor tragedy compared with some of the real ammunition damage. One of the first casualties in the early days of the war was Strete Manor (which had been used as an hotel), a big house at the base of the long winding hill leading up to the village of Strete. Although blamed on the occupying US troops, actually it had been burnt down before the Occupation. However, the stables and cottage on the opposite side of the lane were severely damaged by shellfire but have since been turned into a very charming dwelling house. But the foundations of the manor itself are still as they were when the war ended. Sadly the remains stand in the big gardens at the end of the long coastal road, looking out to sea and waiting for someone to come with a sensible idea of repair. It is understood that the property has changed hands several times since the war ended but that it has now been bought with the intention of re-building the hotel and including some good residential suites.

Torcross at the other end of Slapton Sands had remarkably little damage as far as the exercises went and considering how near it is to the sea great care must have been taken to avoid the village. The stronghold, built by British soldiers early in the war and standing on the Limpet Rocks is now being used by the Natural Environment Research Council as a Unit of Coastal Sedimentation.

The outer perimeter of the Area on the hill tops had experienced the least destruction, being furthest from the coast. Not every house was damaged and some could be lived in again almost immediately. In some cases, however, where there had been heavy shelling, it was actually some years before re-occupation took place.

After the farmers had been helped to get back as soon as possible, the next group to be encouraged to return were the shopkeepers in the villages. Even so, during the autumn of 1944 the strange silence over the land had a curious effect on people in the many still deserted parts. As soon as possible the Information Centre at Stokenham was reopened, the village having suffered little damage save for the church and Church House Inn. Back came the regional commissioner's deputy, Mr Harper, with some of the many helpers who had worked to get the people out; the one difference being that as now there was no call on the various ministries or certain bodies like the RSPCA, the return was a more leisurely affair. It was easier in many other ways too, as there was not the great anxiety and hurry there had been before and the people only came back gradually.

As autumn advanced a few private houses were occupied again; the possessions were brought back as promised free of charge and damage to property paid for, provided application for refund was made. It was perhaps only some feeling about 'not accepting charity' or hesitancy over 'not making a fuss' which deterred one or two families from asking for what was their due, and which resulted later on in a sense of being badly done by. Such an upheaval though was bound to bring some feelings of unfairness or injustice; the left hand not always being aware of what the right hand was doing. It would be unrealistic to suggest that everything went smoothly as the people returned —in such a tremendous uprooting there were bound to be certain anomalies—and although most of the householders settled back again busily enough with the feeling that in their way they had contributed to the war effort, there were those who felt they had just cause to be aggrieved over one thing and another, chiefly recompense. For instance, several letters to the *Kingsbridge Gazette* slated the government for not compensating more generously for damage to property. It was also suggested that more precautions might have been taken against vandalism —the most obvious being that a few Special Constables could have been drafted into the Area after the troops left to help the US sentries keep out the vandals and thieves, for local men would more readily spot an impostor than a US sentry could. But this note of dissension was perhaps surprisingly, only heard from a few; most of the returning people were so glad to be home again, the farmers in particular, that they accepted their compensation grant and got down to work with a will. In fact, one man, living outside the Area and being swayed by just a thought of envy, said 'They was paid such compensation as made proper gen'lmen of some of 'em'. An unfair comment, for the heartaches, the tragedies and sorrows could never be wiped out. It was hard, for instance, on an old farmer, nearer seventy than sixty, to have to give up the farm where he had been his own boss all his life and, at that advanced age, go to work for another man. But what else could he do? he asked. Too old to start up in his farm again, it would be out of the question for him to remain idle, even though he was an old-age pensioner.

The illegal entries which occurred in spite of the sentries who were on guard after D Day until the various parts of the Area were reported free (or as free as possible) from unexploded ammunition, were a problem. Actual householders creeping in to satisfy their anxieties about their homes and properties were understandable, but unhappily many highly suspect characters under the guise of being 'repair men' of one sort or another were able only too easily to enter without question or permit. It seemed to be enough to say 'I'm on a job' and have a van or even a tool bag and no questions were asked. There is no doubt that many just came in 'over the fence' anyway. Once a crisis is over, some people will forget their compassion. In this case the statement that 'the government will put everything right' began to mean 'so help yourself while the going's good', and much wanton damage and downright thieving followed as a natural corollary.

Page 103 (above) *Members of the Headquarters Company, 1st Infantry Division leaving a landing craft*; (below) *American soldiers establishing a beachhead*

Page 104 (above) *A foretaste of the real thing as infantrymen 'hit' the sand to escape the blast of an explosion;* (below) *US soldiers march past the results of shellfire from Navy guns*

One man who had permisison to enter and check his farm arrived at a hilltop to find his van had run out of petrol. Thinking that there might be someone in the nearest village who would be able to help, he coasted downhill, braking as soon as he reached the first group of cottages, then, while he walked in one direction seeking help, he sent his young son who had accompanied him to walk round the other way. And sure enough the farmer had hardly turned the corner when he came upon a lorry standing in the middle of the deserted village with a stranger heaving some articles about inside the vehicle. Yes, he could let the farmer have a gallon of petrol (which was duly paid for), just enough to get him out of the village and to the nearest petrol pump, for the farmer had his petrol permit with him. But the stranger seemed ill-at-ease, he wouldn't explain his reason for being there. In this deserted and silent village the man seemed to bring a curiously secretive air into the proceedings, so that instead of the friendly chat which would be the normal result of such an unexpected meeting in the circumstances, there was an unexplained, furtiveness in his manner. It was not until later, when the farmer had opportunities of hearing stories from others, that he realised that the stranger was there 'just for the gathering'. It also helped to explain why all the little bits of brass in his house, such as door knobs and so on, had unaccountably disappeared.

At least one man saved his house from being despoiled by arriving in the nick of time (with his permit) to see several men descending from a lorry and about to enter the open front door. 'We're taking out the copper boiler in the bathroom and replacing it with a galvanised one,' said one of them with an air of great authority. 'Oh, no you don't,' answered the man. 'This house is mine and I refuse you permission to touch anything.' There was an embarrassed silence and with some muttered remark about a possible mistake, the men got into the lorry without saying another word and drove rapidly away. Nowadays the first thing to have done would have been to take the number of the lorry, but crime and the prevention of it was not so much in the minds of people then. Although many people were so glad to be back again, repairing the tremendous amount of vandalism was a grievous and unnecessary task which had to be faced.

'Why', said one woman, 'should my bathroom hand-basin be smashed to pieces when even the window panes in the room were unbroken? So it couldn't have been done by ammunition.' What pleasure could have been got out of wrecking cupboard doors, larder shelves and suchlike fittings? It was well established that scroungers had deliberately taken items which could be sold secondhand in those days of great shortages, but vandalism as well was unforgivable.

As already mentioned, even in the more secluded parts of the Area it was sometimes quite a long time before a particular house could be made habitable again. For instance, there were signs that the village of Blackawton had been involved in one of the exercises, for although it was high up on the hill it had been knocked about to the extent of several houses being roofless, or partly so, and there was hardly a pane of glass anywhere. The vicarage was no exception: every window broken, no doors left standing, the whole house wide open and in a fearful state of dirt and disorder. The vicar, who had an early permit to view (as Blackawton, being the apex of the triangle, as it were, is right on the outer perimeter) came with his wife, and at the first glimpse of their home their hearts sank. When they had applied at the Kingsbridge Rural District Council offices for the permit and the keys, the man in charge there had smiled gently and said, 'I don't think you'll need keys,' so that they were slightly prepared for trouble, but this really took their breath away. On looking round quickly as they first arrived, they noticed white flags everywhere, so it is to be presumed that a close-up fight had taken place, with the occupying troops in the exercise giving in to those on the opposing side, possibly on receiving orders to do so. There was so much damage to be seen —a shell had gone through the roof—and all looked so utterly neglected and dirty that had it not been for the vicar's wife longing to return to the home she loved, the vicar himself would have asked the bishop to let him remain in the temporary living which had been found for him and where he and his wife had managed to ensconce themselves quite successfully during the past months.

However, before leaving this scene of disaster and confusion they toured the garden, now knee-deep in weeds, and then went to the orchard, hoping to find an early apple or so. Scarcely had they put foot inside, however, when the word seemed to get around and a huge swarm of vicious horse-flies descended upon them in a thick cloud; they literally had to take to their heels and run! Telling the story later to a local man, it was explained to them this way, 'You'm bein' the only livin' critters they flies 'ad seen all summer they was 'oping for a good feast!'

Actually it was several months before the house was cleaned up and repaired sufficiently for the vicar and his wife to return and before word could be given to bring back the stored furniture. It was only then that the state of the well which supplied the house with all necessary water was discovered; there was no mains supply in the village at that time. In some other parts too, cottages had to share a well, though there were private wells also, and in some places a stream running through a village did noble duty. The well at the vicarage was inside the house (common enough in those far-off days when the vicarage was built), and in order to conduct the battle for the house in genuine wartime conditions the soldiers had obviously been instructed that should they be forced to surrender, they must destroy the amenities as far as possible. They had done their job most realistically by contaminating the well, and the pumped-up water was so dirty that the vicar called in the local medical officer of health; the well-cover was removed and a horrifying accumulation of rubbish was disclosed—tyres, oil drums, old bicycles—all kinds of debris. A sample of the water was analysed, reported to be badly polluted, and the vicar and his wife were advised to drink boiled rainwater until the well could be restored. It took a firm of sanitary engineers over three whole days to clean it and remove all the rubbish that had been tipped inside. As a local expression has it, 'it was a real "jakes",' meaning a horrible mess. The vicar said some years later that the Occupation meant a kind of date line in the history of the village —events happened 'before, during or after the Occupation'.

With the exception of the unfortunate village of Blackawton, places up in the hills and away from the coast had little damage; one farmer's wife said that the only alteration in her home was the moving of a picture which she had left in its usual place in the kitchen, not being valuable enough to bother with, she had thought. But the troops, who seemed to have used the house, had taken this picture and hung it up in the parlour, 'to make it more homely' she supposed. It was entitled 'Love's Young Dream'! The people were warned over and over again, when the Evacuation was taking place, not to leave anything behind which they valued in any way but for one reason or another, in all the hurry, mistakes were made. A letter written to a local paper as recently as 1969 said, when commenting upon an article written about the Occupation, 'I wish you could locate the model of a Chinese junk which was taken from my home at this time.'

The few early homecomers of the autumn of 1944 were in great isolation in some places; in fact they sometimes had quite a shock if they saw someone approaching. But as the farms got into working order again and the sound of the cattle in the fields or a distant dog's bark was heard, the busy housewife was able to forget her loneliness as she bustled round her house, cleaning and replacing. However, as one early homecomer said, she had a real feeling of panic when she realised how isolated she actually was. Her husband had left her alone in the house one late afternoon when he departed to fetch some more of their possessions which had been left with a relation in Kingsbridge; 'It soon got dark', she said, 'and I realised that there was no one near for miles and miles', for they were the first back in that particular village. It might seem an odd cause for panic, but it must be remembered that she had lived among close neighbours all her life. There was no post, no butcher, baker or any other shop, no water save that from a nearby stream. Of course there were gangs of men working together on the roads, the farmhouses and other repair jobs, but they were not there later in the day or at weekends, and that was when the heavy silence descended most deeply.

On one occasion a group of partridges, which were not normally seen in this part of the Area, were having a dust bath in the middle of a quiet village street when a nearby cottage window suddenly and noisily opening gave them to realise that this was not the thing to do any more. They left hurriedly and were never seen there again.

Perhaps it was the uncanny silence which encouraged some people to remember omens. A farmer's wife recalled that as their last load of furniture was passing out of the farmyard during the Evacuation, she had suddenly remembered what a gypsy had said to her earlier in that year. Disappointed of a chance to tell a fortune, the gypsy had remarked, sourly, as she was turned away, 'You'll be leaving this place in a hurry one day—you'll see.' 'I've been thinking of that all this morning,' said the farmer's wife, 'how did she know I wonder, for my husband's family has lived here for generations—but she didn't say we'd come back again!'

The scale of agricultural activity gradually increased. The members of one family were able to return to their farm after about ten or eleven months; it was winter time again and not the best moment for moving in, but there had been repairs to be done to the house and some of the barns. A married daughter came to help mother arrange the house once more, and within a few months life seemed to be as before. The land was in a bad state of course, and docks, nettles and all the rest of the quick-growing weeds were abundant. Rabbits had to be snared, and rats also had to be dealt with, but patience and persistence finally removed that worry. The apple orchard was wrecked, for many of the trees had been shelled; however, that was not too serious a problem for the orchard was not large and its crop was not depended upon. It was, naturally enough, distressing to a returning farmer to see the state of his land when making his first inspection after the Occupation, but it was amazing how much was done in a short time with the help of the various agricultural bodies drafted in to lend a hand. The luckiest farmers were those who had been able to stay with friends or relations nearby, especially if they could take some of their stock with them; they were then able to start straight away directly permission was given and if the farmhouse was all right.

Although the entire area had been combed for unexploded ammunition before anyone had official permission to enter, the occasional shell or mine was still being turned up months after D Day. Where the ground was still marshy, for instance, something was occasionally missed by the minesweepers, and although no lives were reported lost due to such a happening, there were many panic-stricken moments when an explosion was heard in or near the field where a farmer was known to be ploughing; sheep were usually the only casualties.

Bit by bit the fields began to assume a more cared-for appearance but it meant very hard work, for as one farmer put it, 'the land had changed its face you see', adding that 'the best and richest ground suffered the most'. It was said that 270 shell holes were counted over 14 acres of pasture in one part. The condition of those farms where the original occupants did not return sank quickly into even greater neglect; however, in such a favourable neighbourhood a farm did not remain empty for long. In the same way as the land had changed its face, as the farmer said, so did the character of some of the homes change as new owners took over empty cottages or shops, and the previously closely-knit village life was never quite the same again. In the villages, sometimes, friendly neighbours could no longer live side by side owing to a bigger cottage being needed by one family, or possibly one cottage having been destroyed or too badly shattered to be rebuilt—the walls of a cob cottage quickly deteriorated, for instance, if a few slates were blown off the roof or a shattered window had let in the weather. Presently there was talk of condemning some of the old cob cottages and, once the war was over, of putting up new council houses. New faces seemed to come from nowhere—another era had begun.

Sometimes very unforeseen happenings prevented a return. One elderly inhabitant had every single pane of glass in the windows of her house broken; these were replaced just before she was due to come back (and wartime glass was not of the best variety in any case) but within a week the whole lot was blown out again by the explosion of a hitherto undiscovered shell. This time there was some structural damage too, so she had to postpone her homecoming for a little longer.

Several people in different places spoke of the boldness of the rats. It was work for a Pied Piper in some parts for they had been in possession for so long that they were a perfect nuisance.

A cottager in one village said that one of them seemed so friendly that she thought it was tapping at the window to be let in; it was some days later that she discovered the truth—the putty securing the glass was mixed with fish oil which the rodents considered a delectable delicacy! Several other people living nearby had the same experience. One man going through his house on his 'permit visit' took the lid off his kitchen boiler to discover a whole nest of young rats inside. The rats were also blamed for gnawing at the stems of fruit bushes in several gardens in one particular village—perhaps they sucked a certain succulence out of the stems. It was very noticeable, said one man, that the damage was only about as far up the stem as a rat could reach. It might be supposed that if they liked the taste of the fruit it would have been more satisfactory to have climbed the branches but it was pointed out that the bushes in most cases could not support the weight of a grown rat.

One farmer was really delighted to find two of his hens still in his yard when he got back. Somehow they had gained access to a sack of mixed corn, overlooked in the rush of going away, had escaped the shelling and missed the attentions of those who came 'a-gathering' too. Moreover he found his beehive with honey and bees intact! But one elderly lady digging a border in her charming but neglected garden, had a less pleasant surprise when she came across a curiously shaped hump in the soil. Wisely she put away her fork and called to a man to come and inspect the object. He lifted it very carefully, uttered one word, 'Naval', laid it tenderly under a bush and called the police; they removed this unexploded shell with the greatest of care and everyone concerned sighed with relief.

Many of those who found a new life in the bigger world outside the Area did not return and there were several who were frankly sorry to come back. One of these postponed his home-coming for over a year; he was a blind man and having made friends in his temporary abode and having learnt his way around his immediate neighbourhood, was really sorry to break up his new life. So he postponed his homecoming until the day after the village pub opened 'so's there'd be some beer in'.

One old man in one of the later parts of the Area to be re-inhabited came to the Information Centre with tears in his eyes to report that his cob cottage was a shambles. It had a stone floor upon which a fire had been lit, using wood which had been torn from the little staircase, cupboard doors and skirtings. It was assumed that the troops had heard vaguely of the disaster of Hallsands, mentioned earlier, and concluded that an empty cob cottage, not looking its best in its desertion, was one of those permanently uninhabited. However, there is an interesting sequel to this tale of vandalism in a cob cottage, for nearly thirty years later a man revisited Torcross, where he had spent a few weeks on a course during 1942. He had then been a subaltern stationed at a brigade headquarters some twenty or thirty miles inland where he had worked for about four months, during which time with a small detachment of men he had been sent down to Slapton Sands to do some practice fighting, to keep them on their toes as it were. The actual beaches were, of course, out of bounds, having already been mined and cordoned off by Coastal Defence, and several of the nearby houses had been emptied of their occupants for fear of enemy landings. Now this man recalls seeing this damaged cob cottage and remembers seeing the remains of the fire which had been built on the stone floor, remembers the torn away staircase railings, the hacked out skirtings and so on, so it is proof that the poor cottage was vandalised long before the US troops arrived. Conscription had already swept up the tramps and other 'drop-outs' so that it is difficult to know who could have been so foolish. A brief and probably correct answer could be naughty boys.

On the other hand, a cottage not very far away from this had been painted white inside just before it was evacuated, and that gave an artist among the US troops a wonderful opportunity to display his talent when off duty. He did such beautiful murals on the white walls that afterwards the occupant of the cottage was continually being asked if she would let people in to see them. Not to be beaten, another US soldier composed some lines of poetry with which he adorned the walls in another room. Only these were in a distinctly different mood—the effect of reading this effort usually produced a loud guffaw or a ribald comment or two! This particular cottage was lucky, but regrettably there were several others whose walls were treated with rough drawings, remarks and verses, from the slightly vulgar to the downright pornographic.

There is a row of picturesque cottages right on the sands facing the sea, and the owner of one, having obtained her 'permit to view', went down to the deserted beach to inspect the little house; it was high tide and very peaceful. She was upstairs when, in the stillness of the afternoon, she heard a lorry draw up on the road behind. There was the tramp of soldiers' feet as they crunched their way over the shingle to the water's edge, then, knowing that our own troops were still looking for washed-up ammunition she concluded, knowing very little about such military matters, that each of the men standing in a row was holding a mine detector. Standing by an open window, she called to her friend downstairs, 'Oh, come and look at these brave men.' One of them heard her and half turned round and she realised that they were not holding mine detectors but simply obeying nature's call. She backed away from the window in a hurry.

One family had a delightful homecoming. They lived in a pretty house up in the hills, untouched save for a broken window or two. But of the three children, two were away at boarding school when their home was evacuated while the youngest, a child of barely four years old, could scarcely remember the house. It was November before their furniture was brought back and the house spruced up and put into order in time for the Christmas holidays. Father had a few days' leave, the schoolchildren arrived back just a day before him, and the little one, shown into the bedroom which he was to share again with his big brother, looked out of the window at the view and was actually silent for a moment. Then he turned to his mother and said simply, 'It's bleautiful' and 'bleautiful' became a much used family word for years afterwards.

One man and his wife, who came to live in the Area before the war, had a son, George, who was destined to go to the Royal Naval College at Dartmouth, relatively a few miles away. During those early years he was able to cycle home on short leaves, and the tinkling of bicycle bells would herald his arrival, always accompanied by a friend or two. However when war came, the college, being in a conspicuous position high up on the hill above Dartmouth, was hastily moved to a temporary country home at Eaton Hall in Cheshire. That was a shock, but when the parents discovered later that their home was actually inside the area to be evacuated, they experienced, with all the others, an even greater shock. By this time George was out of college and had been at sea for some weeks. No letters had reached him and the first he heard of the Evacuation was when his ship docked at a home port at the end of December. During his few days' leave he accompanied his parents to a small inland town where they had been lucky enough to find accommodation in a little nondescript hotel; but instead of the lovely view from his bedroom window, the trim lawn, the trees and the sea beyond, George could only see depressing roof tops and chimney pots. No one mentioned the old spaniel, and his possessions were all carefully packed away; it was all so different from the few days' respite that he had visualised.

Actually his parents were able to be back in their home again by the Christmas following D Day as the house was untouched and they were among the few lucky ones who could walk straight in. Only George wasn't with them this time. One lovely morning in early summer, while in convoy, he had gone down with his ship in mid-Atlantic.

One inhabitant had the extreme joy of finding some treasures which had been put away in a wonderful hiding place where they had lain undisturbed all through the fighting and subsequent looting. The lucky finder had been brought up in a charming and rather old house which had been adapted and altered from time to time, and during the early twenties a cupboard had been built against an outer wall in her bedroom. As the space between this cupboard floor and the ceiling of the room below was fairly deep, the floor boards were cut to the length of the cupboard and replaced but not nailed down; the hidey-hole thus formed was lined with zinc and there was a marvellous secret spot in which to hide her childish treasures. The cupboard floor was then given a strip of fitted linoleum so there was nothing to suggest to the eye that the floor boards concealed such a space. By the time World War 11 began the little girl had grown up and was in a responsible job in London. In 1943 her mother had died, suddenly, only a few weeks before the news of the Evacuation was announced and, as she was unable to get more leave so soon after her mother's funeral, her father was forced, with help from the WVS, to pack up the house without her.

However, when during the September of 1944 a permit was issued to her father to inspect the house, she was able to accompany him down to the South Hams. There was certain damage done by nearby explosions but nothing that could not be put right easily enough—broken window panes, plaster torn off walls, but on the whole they were agreeably surprised, having heard from friends of far worse destruction. Then, more in a mood of nostalgia than anything else, she drifted into her old bedroom, looked at the cupboard and remembered the secret space. Taking up the strip of linoleum, she lifted the boards and what a sight met her eyes! It was packed with treasures—pieces of family silver she had not seen for years, most of her mother's jewellery, neatly placed in their cases, bundles of valuable old letters and various other small treasures, including some little pieces of precious china. Rushing to her father, she bade him come and see what she had found. He was dumbfounded; he knew his wife had packed away much of their silver when the war started but in the sudden upheaval of having to clear out so soon after her death, he had let several boxes and chests go into store without opening them to check their contents to see if anything was missing. 'There were three or four boxes all roped or padlocked,', he said, 'but I think she must have put this stuff in here when the war actually started. I'd no idea it was here; but I do know it's worth a lot of money.'

That was a most unusual case, though, for however carefully packed most people's possessions were, a good many people lost something; not necessarily anything important—a box of kitchen utensils or perhaps some china was broken. On the other hand some seemed to feel it was a small price to pay for the tremendous experience of helping to increase the know-how which had helped to save so many lives on the Normandy beaches. One woman said she had lost a box containing family photographs which were irreplaceable, but that she didn't regret her wedding photos for she had always felt that they did not do justice to either herself or her husband!

A bright spot lay in the splendid and generous gifts from both the Canadian and American Red Cross; both societies sent enormous consignments of many types of household goods especially for the returning inhabitants of the Area. What matter if someone had lost her favourite teapot, there would almost certainly be one in one of these great cases. There were such practical articles as door-mats, saucepans, tins of paint of a quality unknown in Britain at the time, cups and saucers, brooms, scrubbing brushes, buckets—the list is never ending and those on the receiving end were really touched, until it came to dealing out the bedspreads. Some of these were prettier than others and more than one flash of spiteful jealousy was recorded by those tireless WVS helpers who once more were on hand to help, welcome home, and smooth down little arguments. A big barn was offered in which to unpack and sort these very welcome consignments, and much trouble was taken to ensure that the articles were handed out as fairly as possible.

Some of the older generation had been living very simply until World War 11 broke out. One man and his wife were found accommodation about thirty miles away in a rather big house in which they were given a job as caretakers. The owners were both 'war working' and this seemed a better alternative to leaving the house empty. The man worked in the garden and during the time they were there he was able to get it into good shape again while his wife looked after the house. They were among those who really enjoyed the time spent away and the man quickly took the fancy of those who liked to listen to him talking. He had come from a remote hamlet where electricity had not yet arrived. Over his evening pint at the local, after his return, he caused much quiet fun by describing how 'you jest push a little button and the house is afire!'

And so gradually the Area came to life again, its villages and its farming flourished anew. The people came to forget the loneliness, the eerie, depressing silence of the first few months of their homecoming, when the farmers' wives had felt they were not in the world at all once their husbands and sons had gone outside to work. As one of them said, when looking back on those early days: ''Twas terrible quiet, but 'twas better after a few weeks when the cottages nearby began to fill up, and then the shops in the village. Yes, 'twas better then, and I soon got some good hens in the yard and they cackled loud enough to drive out any quiet!'

SIX
The Churches

AS SOON AS POSSIBLE—MID-AUGUST IN FACT—DOWN from Exeter came the firm which had so carefully dismantled, sandbagged and sent away the church treasures for safety. This time there was much more to do as some of the churches were badly damaged and required much attention to put them right, but on the other hand the need for urgency had gone. Also the men concerned were able to stay nearer the Area this time, only going home at weekends: the War Agricultural Executive Committee was using the big rectory at Charlton as a hostel for land workers so room was found for them there, and the Women's Voluntary Service drivers took them to and fro daily.

All things considered, the harm done to the churches, with two exceptions, was not as great as had been feared. The church at Strete for instance, built only during the last century, seems to have been untouched. The practice ammunition does not appear to have hurt this village as much as a passing enemy plane which put a bomb right into the middle of it. One man in the village street was knocked out for a moment by the blast and, on recovering, found he was lying on top of a small boy. They were both unhurt but the man's house was damaged. So also was the charming old forge which, not so long before the war began, had been converted into a reading room and a small village hall; it was completely demolished by the same bomb. The open space is now used as a car park by the village inn, The King's Arms.

Stokenham Church was damaged by an explosion which occurred just outside when, during one of the practices, a stray shell blasted a hole in the nearby Church House Inn, knocking down a wall and at the same time taking a piece out of the church roof. The south aisle was badly damaged and all the stained glass in the windows on that side was blown out and had to be replaced by plain glass. The actual structural work was carried out by a local builder when he repaired the Church House Inn. There is a sanctuary ring on the west door which bears the date 1636, and which must have been on a still earlier door. This survived, luckily. The church was of Norman origin though the present building seems to have been begun in the early fourteenth century and a list of all the vicars up to the present day hangs from a pillar in the nave giving Geoffrey de Farnham as the first incumbent; the church was restored twice during the last century. Standing as it does not far from the sea, it is fortunate that this very beautiful old building did not have more damage done to its structure during the Occupation. When the latter was ended the firm from Exeter came again, as to the other churches, to replace the beautifully carved screen, take away the sandbags and generally tidy up, and it is now in excellent order.

East Allington Church appears to have been untouched; situated far up in the hills it was too remote to have been reached by the seaborne fighting and its beauty and peace seem to have been undisturbed.

Blackawton Church, however, was a very different matter and was indeed a sorry sight. The really sad thing about this church is that so much of the damage which was done could not in all honesty be laid on the doorstep of the troops involved in the exercises, in spite of the story put about that they were to blame. So many unauthorised people came into the Area after D Day who had literally no business there at all, that it is impossible to apportion the blame; but Blackawton Church certainly had unfair treatment. Of what use the barbed wire, the bishop's notice and the locked doors? 'Out of bounds' notices were torn down, doors left swinging open, and there was practically no glass left anywhere. This could have been the result of blast, but blast did not account for the cigarette butts which were nearly knee deep on the floor, especially round the organ, nor the empty bottles and fragments of glasses. Hymn and prayer books, left neatly stacked (though actually they should have been removed) were strewn everywhere and, worst of all, the organ pipes had been dismantled and thrown around, including some which were even out in the churchyard. Blackawton at that time was one of the places to which electricity had not yet been brought and the church had been lit by forty really good oil lamps; every lamp disappeared. When it came to recompense, a mere £50 was paid for organ repairs, which seems trifling by today's money values; nevertheless it was sufficient then to put the organ back into proper working order. The vicar was convinced that a party had taken place inside the church and that the organ pipes had been used as a version of the 'penny whistle'.

The little thirteenth-century church of Sherford, also tucked away in the hills, was not harmed. As a matter of fact some of the delicate and brittle carving in the screen was so worm ridden, said the foreman who had to dismantle it, that after it had been treated and carefully repaired it went back in a better state than it had been in before it was removed. In his opinion, all the woodwork here was in a very dilapidated condition, but when it was put back not only had the weak parts been repaired but the chancel door had been made to open and shut properly and the whole building put into good order; so that it could be said, in this case, that replacing came to mean restoration. Not one of the biggest churches, it has great charm and it is undoubtedly one of the treasures of the neighbourhood. The walls at the west end of the building, however, were deeply covered with moss owing to extreme damp but, now that a benefactor has generously given an electric central-heating apparatus which should in time discourage all such growth, it is to be hoped that no serious harm has been done to the structure of this ancient and interesting building.

Slapton Church had a direct hit by a shell which destroyed the south wall and created an enormous amount of destruction. One small stained-glass window from the vestry was found in the churchyard, fortunately undamaged. The wall and windows had to be rebuilt and, in this connection, a local inhabitant stated that the original stone which was blown out had come in the first place from Normandy, thus making a curious link with the reason for the Occupation. The roof has been built in three domed or vaulted shapes, the centre one over the nave and the high altar being loftier than the two side ones. As it was the south wall which was damaged, the roof here was covered with tarpaulin for many months before it could be put right, and villagers said it blew up and down like a ship's sails when the wind got up. The south aisle was boarded off for about three years and when it rained the roof 'was like a sieve'. Dust from the shattered masonry covered the interior of the church almost as deeply as a carpet; it was swept up again and again until finally the foreman got down on his hands and knees and scrubbed the floor from end to end 'right proper', wearing out several scrubbing brushes in the process. Another difficulty was the quantity of steel splinters which were embedded in the wooden pews on the damaged side of the church. They were tiny and extremely sharp so that, although almost invisible, they could do great damage to the clothes of worshippers using the pews. The only way to make quite sure that all were removed was to run the hand along the wood and then dig them out piece by piece. In many cases the holes had to be replaced with little bits of wood and polished in.

It seems a pity that what once must have been an imposing tomb, though only part of its cover stone existed even before the war, should have received further damage. All that now remains is a fragment of stone with the words 'Lady Judith' on it and this has been built into the restored wall. She was the Lady Judith Hawkins, the wife of Sir Richard Hawkins, son of Sir John Hawkins of Spanish War fame. Sir Richard was captured and put into a Spanish prison and although his father gave £3,000—a goodly sum in those days—he was not released for ten years, when he returned unannounced and to the great surprise of everyone, says the legend. He died in 1622 but his wife survived him until 1629. The legend also states that the Lady Judith was a bit of a character and on the few occasions when she condescended to attend church, two pages went in front to lay strips of carpet down the sloping church path, in case she should come into contact with the mud that abounded there. There is, of course, no means of proving or disproving a legend of such antiquity, but if there is any truth in it at all, the effect of the carpet strips must have been very grand especially as it probably only happened when the sun was shining.

Also in Slapton Church are two delightful figures, carved in wood, of a knight and his lady, which are wonderfully preserved. The figures are separate and are kneeling; they are only two or three feet high and with folded hands they face each other, placed on a shelf near the Lady Judith stone. There is neither date nor name to identify them. Of course, all portable treasures such as these figures were taken away to safety by the churchwardens in 1943 and in some cases this meant that they were being hidden for the second time in their history. For, during the Civil War, Cromwell made extensive campaigns around the south-west of England including Devon, encouraging his men between bouts of fighting to find and remove anything of value—silver, brass, any 'Popish' treasure they could come across—and so many a lectern, crucifix or candlestick lay hidden in a secret place, sometimes underground for several years until, at the Restoration, it became safe for the vicar and churchwardens to produce and display them again. There are, for instance, several Elizabethan chalices and patens among the churches in the Area which had to suffer this indignity for the second time, though probably it was not considered necessary to put them underground on this occasion.

Like Stokenham, Slapton Church also has a sanctuary ring. It is fastened on to the north door and is unusual in that it is shaped like a horseshoe; it is very old and fortunately it, too, survived the shelling intact. The idea of church sanctuary is an ancient one: and if a criminal or other fugitive who was being pursued could get as far as the church door and just grasp the ring the church would grant him sanctuary—for a certain period.

Early in the year following D Day, while the repairs to the churches were still in full swing, there was a very heavy fall of snow. This does not often happen in the South Hams and snow rarely remains on the ground for long, but this came at the beginning of a weekend and the lorry which would have taken the church workers back to Exeter was unable to get through to their lodgings at Charlton. So the men were preparing to trudge through the snow to the ferry at Dartmouth, intending to cross the river to get the train at Kingswear, when the news came by phone that the vicar of Slapton had died and was being brought back to his churchyard to be buried that very afternoon —by which time, it was presumed, the roads would be easier to negotiate. Suddenly the foreman realised that he had locked up the church very securely for the weekend, which he always did to make sure that their tools were safe from interlopers, and that the funeral party would be unable to get inside. So off he set to cover six miles of snow on foot to open up the doors, only to discover when the mourners arrived that there had been no intention of going into the church itself.

By and large, then, the churches of the Area came out of the Exodus a little on the credit side, for there is no doubt that much infected fifteenth-century woodcarving, some of which was found in most of the churches, was caught in the nick of time and saved from worse woodworm damage by the care it received. The delicate pieces of the carved screens which were carefully restored and replaced after the Occupation now stand just as if nothing but kindly old age had touched them; while the whole of the woodwork has been treated with a modern solution to kill woodworm which should guarantee immunity for some years to come. Unhappily the wood beetle travels from one building to another, and once a neighbourhood gets one badly infected piece of wood, be it in a barn, house or church, then it is not long before similar damage spreads to any nearby wood which has a soft spot. It will be necessary in the years to come to keep a strict watch on those delicate church carvings which have been so well repaired, in case woodworm may crop up again. There can be so little 'body' left in some of the wood that this may need more skilful attention sooner than was anticipated when it was put back in all its glory. Roof structures, indeed any part of these ancient buildings, may yet show signs of breaking away or cracking due to hidden wartime damage.

Chancel screens in the fifteenth century usually followed a

pattern, and the ones in Devon were particularly lovely. Delicate carvings along the top were connected to the base by vertical railings, while the base was a sort of barrier divided into narrow panels roughly three or four feet high, separated from each other by a wooden frame; then each panel was usually painted with the figure of a saint. That was all very well until Cromwell's men came along. Curiously enough they did not destroy the beautiful chancel screens but they could not stand the portraits of the saints. Each figure was blanked out by a splash of plain paint, and so it remained until, mostly in the last century, a few new paintings were done by artists using good colours and, as far as possible, historical accuracy with regard to costumes. Whether the saints so portrayed were the same as the original ones is a matter of conjecture. But in a few instances, the doors in the centre of the screen and the panels on each side of the doors had the dirty, colourless paint cleaned off (in much the same way as an oil painting is restored), showing the original faint suggestion of the figure underneath, and on one or two adjoining panels new pearl-grey paint was applied to show what it all looked like before, and after, Cromwell's men had done their worst. Many chancel screens in Devon have been partially restored in this way as well as those in the Area; possibly the most unusual paintings in the South Hams are to be found in Blackawton, for there the paintings are mostly of curious faces rather than the conventional figures of saints. One or two panels have had to be repaired with new wood where a large piece was knocked out in 1944, but in these cases the repaired part has wisely been left unpainted.

It is sometimes asked why so many churches have a 'church house' built alongside, and nowadays very often used as an inn. It is believed by some that the house or cottage was built to shelter the workmen who were constructing or altering the church; sometimes the erection of a big church would go on over two generations of workmen. In the early sixteenth century these 'church houses' increased quickly in numbers for by then it was realised how useful they could be in acting as the 'parish room'. Many of these houses have become lost amidst the villages which grew up around them, though many were preserved down the years as shelters for worshippers, who often came from a long way off and needed somewhere to go between services and eat the food they had brought with them. In time they became the responsibility of the feoffees and were used for parish meetings, church feasts and so on, or occasionally for the brewing of ale and baking of bread. Sometimes they became village schools or housed the poor of the village. So the inn of today, like the Church House Inn at Stokenham, can often be the descendant of the original church house.

It was the custom in medieval times for some rich person to leave a sum of money to the church to provide small gifts to the poor of the parish. It usually took the form of a once-a-year distribution of bread, or some such necessary help for poor families. The instructions were often accompanied by dire threats of some disaster if the procedures were not carried out. In Blackawton Church, for example, the interesting old tomb of the Rev Richard Spark, railed around for greater protection and dated 1700, carries a notice explaining that a sum of money was left to the church authorities to provide bread for the villagers; it is mostly given to the children nowadays. A copy of Richard Spark's will hangs on the railing. This appears on the tomb:

All you that here God's word Repaire
Pray keep my Toombe in Good Repaire
And you that of my Bread doe eat
See that it Stand Both Clean and Neat
For whiles My Toombe here Safely Stands
In Peace you shall Enjoy my Lands
But if you Let it to Decay
My Alms from you shall Fall away.
Henceforth Let no Man move those Bones
That Buried Lie under these Stones.

In the church porch, incidentally, hangs a beautifully hand-written prayer which, it is stated, was once painted on the wall. It was lost during the traumatic days of 1944 when it became too dirty or defaced to save when the porch had to be cleaned up. But the wording was remembered, copied and framed. Stokenham Church, incidentally, holds a will dated 1708, made by Andrew Jeffery who lived in the village and who left a sum of money whereby three poor freemen were to be provided with clothing. Probably an overcoat, perhaps a jacket of sorts or even boots, may have been distributed once a year. Apparently the charity is still able to carry out these instructions but nowadays the gift is given in money.

So the churches of the South Hams continue much as they have done for hundreds of years. The war destroyed so many historical, ancient and beautiful churches up and down the country that the people in the Occupied Area of South Devon may congratulate themselves that, in spite of the risks and dangers of those harrassing six months, not to mention the tip and run raids, no worse catastrophe came to their precious heritage.

SEVEN
Aftermath

WHO WOULD GUESS, WHEN LOOKING AT THE COASTLINE today that, during those six months thirty years ago, such a holocaust had taken place on the beaches of the South Hams? The shore of the Area now looks much the same as it did before World War II, apart from the fact that one or two prominent buildings such as the Royal Sands Hotel are missing. But that the ridged beach at Slapton and the Ley behind look much as they have done for hundreds of years is due to the vigilance of those who own the foreshore; they even succeed to some extent in keeping that modern destroyer, the motor car, under control. When summer weather prevails there is nothing more beautiful in South Devon than Start Bay, with the ever-changing blues of the sea, the equally lovely blues of the sky above, a slight suggestion of haze veiling the horizon—or better still a sharp demarcation line—all enclosed in the semi-circle from Dartmouth to Start Point. On a clear, bright day such different shades of blue from the sky and sea can be magnificent though, during the great winter gales when sky and sea become a relentless and menacing grey, the landscape is just as fascinating. But the sea can be dangerous then and its wild beauty is best watched from a point of safety; it is no wonder that people flock to these shores.

But it is to be wondered if many of those who visit the beaches realise what dramatic and often tragic scenes were enacted, not only where they are sitting or strolling, but also on the hills which rise up behind them. Perhaps some of the visitors may occasionally look at the large granite obelisk which stands about midway along the road from Torcross to Strete Gate on the edge of Slapton Sands, but there are so many memorial stones in towns and villages all over the country erected to the memory of the men and women who gave their lives in the great fight for freedom, that they tend to be taken for granted. This, however, is a memorial obelisk with a difference—it is to the living, who, within a brief space of six weeks, gave up their homes and farmlands in order to contribute to the training of what could be described as 'new' soldiers in a world war; 'new' in as much as the bulk of them had never experienced live ammunition before and that so many of them, in any case, were almost straight out of civilian life. When the great winds blow and a gale gets up and sweeps inland from the English Channel, it is easy to imagine those days of practice fighting. Sometimes the rain will come in from the sea almost at right angles, like flying arrows might, and then one can almost see the unforgettable scenes of their agonies of fighting. The gales which blow are sometimes so fierce that, quite recently, a woman waiting near the obelisk to catch the bus which runs along the coastal road, remarked to another would-be passenger, 'I wish they'd put up a shelter here instead of this memorial stone.'

The ceremony of unveiling this memorial presented by the United States of America was held on 24 July 1954 and invitations were sent to all those householders who had returned to

The Lord Lieutenant of Devon, Colonel The Right Honourable
The Earl Fortescue, K.G., P.C., C.B., O.B.E., M.C.,
requests the pleasure of the company of

Major C. W. Davis.

at the United States of America's Memorial at Slapton Sands
On Saturday, the 24th July, 1954, at 3 p.m.
and
Captain W. G. Crawford, D.S.C., R.N., *requests the pleasure of your company at a Reception to be held at the Britannia Royal Naval College, Dartmouth, at 4.30 p.m. to meet the Supreme Commander, Allied Forces in Europe, General Alfred M. Gruenther.*

R.S.V.P.
Captain's Secretary,
Britannia Royal Naval College, Dartmouth.

P.T.O.

Invitation to the unveiling of the memorial on Slapton Sands

their homes by the Lord Lieutenant of Devon, Earl Fortescue. After the ceremony, Captain W. G. Crawford, RN, gave a reception at the Britannia Royal Naval College, Dartmouth, for the guests to meet the Supreme Commander Allied Forces in Europe, General Alfred M. Gruenther. Invitations were also issued to representatives of the official groups and voluntary bodies who had worked during the Evacuation and return.

The wording on the stone reads as follows:

THIS MEMORIAL
WAS PRESENTED BY THE UNITED STATES
ARMY AUTHORITIES TO THE PEOPLE OF THE
SOUTH HAMS WHO GENEROUSLY LEFT
THEIR HOMES AND THEIR LANDS TO
PROVIDE A BATTLE PRACTICE AREA FOR
THE SUCCESSFUL ASSAULT IN NORMANDY
IN JUNE 1944

THEIR ACTION RESULTED IN THE SAVING OF MANY HUNDREDS OF LIVES AND CONTRIBUTED IN NO SMALL MEASURE TO THE SUCCESS OF THE OPERATION. THE AREA INCLUDED THE VILLAGES OF BLACKAWTON, CHILLINGTON, EAST ALLINGTON, SLAPTON, STOKENHAM, STRETE, AND TORCROSS, TOGETHER WITH MANY OUTLYING FARMS AND HOUSES

Unfortunately the village of Sherford was omitted from this list as it was bracketed ecclesiastically with Stokenham, and there does not seem room among the rest of the lettering in which to add it.

Although the obelisk has been much appreciated by the local inhabitants, occasional visitors do not seem always to understand. During the summer of 1970, for instance, a man from another part of the country carefully read the inscription, then turned to a local bystander saying, 'But this didn't really happen, did it?' He should have talked with some more of the dwellers in the Area and heard a little about the difficulties, the tragedies and the destruction. In July 1971, moreover, that visitor, had he been there to see, would have had a sharp reminder of those Occupation days for, while the ground was being bulldozed during the construction of the new central car park on the sands at the very spot where the Royal Sands Hotel once stood, an unexploded anti-tank mine was uncovered, one of those which was placed there by the Coastal Defence in the early days of the war. Dartmouth police came to help the Kingsbridge Rural Council workmen clear the beach for 500 yards each side and about 150 cars were ordered to move. A Royal Naval bomb disposal squad from Plymouth came to explode the mine which left a hole of about fifteen feet. It is interesting to reflect how many holidaymakers must have walked over the top of that mine since it was put there all those years ago!

The foreshore at Slapton is owned by the Whitley Trust and

it was decided after the war not to rebuild the Royal Sands Hotel as the congestion of traffic was solid enough in the summer in any case, and an inn would only have increased this out of all proportion. Cars have been running off the road and parking on the shingle ever since the war ended. Sometimes a car would sink a little and not be able to grip firm ground again when the owner wished to move off, so that it had to be towed out, and the continual wear and tear was beginning to do real harm to the shingle and grass verge and to the flowers growing thereon, some of which are very unusual.

There had been an idea earlier in this century of buying the property consisting of the Ley and its surroundings, draining away all the water and filling it in to road level so as to build a row of houses all along its length of two and a half miles, facing the road and sea. Fortunately the Whitley Trust was able to step in and acquire both this land and the Ley, with the result that not only is it still an undisturbed beauty spot but it has been the means of preserving so much in the way of birds, flowers, fish, insects, waterfowl and so on, becoming a very important nature reserve (see map, page 29). The Slapton Field Centre, which has its headquarters in Slapton village, is doing invaluable work here. It is one of several such stations in the country where wild life in all its forms is studied, preserved and duly catalogued; a fascinating place where the work brings together much in the way of scientific research and teaching. Scientists and university staff visit regularly, students and groups from schools are able to come to study for a week or so at a time, and an observation hut to house a small independent group of people for a few days has been built just above the Ley itself. It was constructed in the same year that the Field Centre was opened but was not ready for occupation until 1961. A small wooden structure, it will sleep up to six people at a time and is designed for those who wish to study bird life for short periods. It is fully equipped with the necessary mist nets, official rings and a balance for weighing the trapped birds before releasing them again. It provides a simple life for its occupants but one full of interest for those who really make a study of ornithology.

Among the plants which are so carefully protected, the outstanding one is strapwort (*Corrigiola littoralis*). Slapton is now the only place in Britain where it still grows and it appears there in varying quantities from year to year. Other carefully preserved treasures include the small flowered buttercup, lesser birdsfoot trefoil, pennyroyal mint, thorn apple, sea radish, sea bindweed, yellow horned poppy, sea spurge and bogbean, besides many other well known favourites. In order to preserve the grass verges as much as possible, short wooden posts have been driven into the ground at the edge of parts of the road bordering the shingle so that some at least of the wild flowers can be secure from motor cars, though there is space for parking at Strete Gate and at Torcross. Except at Torcross the Ley side of the road is too uneven and overgrown for cars to venture to park on it. The new central car park on the shingle will take many cars and coaches.

As the Ley is one of the largest freshwater lakes in the southwest, it is brimming over with wild life. It varies in width from 200 feet to over 1,000 feet across, giving plenty of space for variety. Not only do clouds of flies, midges, gnats and butterflies hover over it but out of the 41 species of dragonfly which have been catalogued as living in this country, no fewer than 17 have been checked and counted in the Slapton neighbourhood. The Ley which has only been known to freeze over very rarely, is also said to be the water in Devon most frequented by freshwater ducks, while most of the Devon coot breed here. Reed warblers, sedge warblers and reed buntings use the wayside vegetation for breeding while the linnet, whitethroat and stonechat are to be found nesting in the brambles and gorse, evidently looking upon such prickly vegetation as protection. The skylark and meadow pipit favour the rough grass while a few pairs of ringed plover breed on the sands. These are just examples of the many birds that bring ornithologists to Slapton Ley. Rarer species also come occasionally, such migrants being of immense value to the extremely interesting work done by the Field Centre.

With the new menace of oil pollution in our seas, Slapton Ley Centre, in an arrangement with the Nature Conservancy, is to offer emergency research in the event of a major oil spill in its area. This was decided upon in 1970 after the tanker *Pacific Glory* had released very large quantities of oil and the Centre, together with the RSPCA, had dealt with many oiled sea birds.

But housing developers and nature conservationists are not the only people who have been interested in the Slapton area since the end of the war. In 1961 the film company of Daryl F. Zanuck Productions Incorporated, asked permission from Kingsbridge Rural Council to film a landing of 500 men from invasion craft in Start Bay. The company had been intending to make a film of the preparation for D Day and it was suggested that in order to have it as realistic as possible they should use the actual beach where so many exercises had taken place. But Kingsbridge Rural Council had already spent much time, money and effort in removing the litter left from the camping and caravaning of the previous summer, and when it was learned that the filming would go on from the beginning of June until the end of August—the actual peak of the holiday season—the answer was obviously 'No'. However, before answering the request, the council asked for the views of the Whitley Trust and also those of the Field Studies Council. Both of them emphatically answered 'No' also, having in mind the verges, so full of unusual and special wild flowers which would almost completely disappear with the tramping to and fro of 500 men and all the necessary paraphernalia of cameras and vehicles during a period of three months. It would have practically put a stop to part of the Field Centre's work.

However, two years later, in May 1963, some 400 men from 43 Commando, based at Stonehouse Barracks, Plymouth, raced up the same strip of shingle beach, having arrived in landing craft from a battleship to take up combat positions on the road opposite. There were also frogmen, manning canoes. But they made only two landings before they quietly re-embarked and returned to Plymouth, having done little or no damage. It was a rehearsal for an exercise named 'Awex', to be carried out in Normandy on a beach which had been named 'Utah' during the 1944 invasion and was presumably a combined exercise with the French. Watching the exercise with a critical eye born of his experience on the same South Hams beach twenty years before was an officer of the Amphibious Training Unit. He said it was quite uncanny to see the landing on this spot: 'Even the weather was similar.' It is possible that this particular exercise was seen by many people from one position or another, in spite of the weather, but it is to be wondered if any of them visualised as clearly as that observing officer the flying bullets, the shells and the men who were wounded or even killed on that now peaceful stretch of shingle.

There is scarcely a sign of damage to be seen in the Area now unless one knows exactly where to look for it. The broken and dead trees have been felled and only the occasional distorted or misshapen one is still there as a reminder of the leafless and twisted trees which were to be seen for several years on the hillsides. The dead ones were cut out as soon as the more important farming tasks left time, but it was quickly discovered that they were too full of shrapnel to be any use for firewood. One poor old woman, sitting in front of her fire on a cold evening with her skirts pulled up over her knees, suddenly received so many pieces of shrapnel in her knees and legs that the hospital to which she was taken had to remove sixty splinters. Not a soul in the entire county wanted to have wood fires afterwards for a long while unless they knew exactly where the wood had come from.

Among the characteristics of the neighbourhood what remains in the mind as the most outstanding? Perhaps the many beautifully built walls of small flat pieces of slate which, cemented neatly together, form a smooth and interesting surface, sometimes low, sometimes many feet in height. They surround gardens and large farmyards and must have taken a very long time to build, though they were mostly put up in the days when time was not so important. Slate is used a good deal as it is found in the district and many an entrance to a drive or a large farm has pillars on each side of the gate, completely circular, several feet in diameter and with a sloping top, all built of this same slate; in this case small pieces are used but nevertheless the pillars are solid throughout. Also many house walls are hung with overlapping slates, beginning at the roof edge and running halfway down the outer wall, which gives a charming effect as well as protecting the wall underneath. The long walls leading up from Strete Gate to the village of Strete were originally constructed in this way but when the 'giant's bites' were repaired they were mostly built of local granite and topped with the traditional 'cock and hen' finish—that is, one big pointed stone standing on end, then a small, neat flatter one, and so on, all in the same type and colour. It is possible to pick out the repaired 'giant's bites' even today but generally speaking they are passed by unnoticed. Most of the damage was done to the wall nearer the sea.

The return of the exiled inhabitants brought a new outlook to compete with the old traditions. More up-to-date agricultural machinery was gradually bought as it became available after the stringencies of wartime. The actual moving away into new surroundings, meeting new people who had perhaps a slightly different outlook on life in general and on farming in particular made quite a change in the lives of some. Many people are just a little sorry, however, that the soft, blurred dialect of Devon is gradually dying out, save among the older people or those in more remote spots. Radio, television and the incursion of visitors from other parts of the country have all helped in this; and it is not only the accent which is fast disappearing but all those delightful phrases and expressions which used to make listening to a truly Devon character such a pleasure.

To show that, unlike his predecessor, the modern South Hams dweller is quite prepared to experiment with new ideas, in 1956 two fishing boats were observed, not very far out from the shore, using the up-to-date method of big lights in order to attract the fish to the nets. Each boat had two very powerful arc-lights on stands at each side, and the boats were not very far away from each other. It is a method which works in some places but apparently it did not catch on in Start Bay for there is no sign of it still being used today. Something of the same idea, however, is being used on land. Quite recently, a visitor to Torcross whose bedroom window looked straight down the length of the sands towards the village of Strete, saw his room suddenly lit up in the middle of the night by a powerful light coming from the wooded slopes on the hills near Strete village. Enquiries led to the information that it was probably rabbit catchers at work using powerful lights to paralyse or fascinate their victims, making it easy to shoot or capture them. It seems curious to find such an unsporting method so near what is a real conservationist district centred on the Slapton Field Centre.

'Normandy' has left some impression on the South Hams. The tiny quay at Salcombe, only a few miles outside the occupied Area, was used to embark some of the US troops participating in the D Day attack, and now this plaque, headed by a US star, is displayed on a wall:

NORMANDY WAY
SO NAMED TO COMMEMORATE THE MEN
OF THE UNITED STATES NAVY
WHO PASSED THIS WAY TO EMBARK
FOR THE NORMANDY BEACHES,
THERE TO ASSAULT THE ENEMY
ON 'D' DAY, TUESDAY, THE 6TH OF JUNE, 1944.
AN AMPHIBIOUS FORCE OF 66 SHIPS
OF THE UNITED STATES NAVY,
WITH MANY AUXILIARY VESSELS,
SAILED FROM THE PORT OF SALCOMBE
ON THE 4TH OF JUNE, 1944, TO TAKE PART
IN THIS GREAT ENTERPRISE.

Also, one of the village inns up in the hills of the Area has been renamed the Normandy Arms, and to add to the atmosphere the walls of the two little bars are hung with photos and paintings of the beaches invaded on D Day, together with photos and caricatures of such important personalities as Sir Winston Churchill, General Eisenhower, etc.

Obviously the South Hams, as other parts of the countryside, have lost some institutions which were once part of the rural way of life. Fairly recently a Blackawton parish meeting was protesting about the replacement of the village policeman by a visiting 'panda-car'—it was reported that there had been an increase in thieving and wanton damage in Blackawton, including thefts from the post office and the church. That poor church! One would have thought it had suffered enough during the Occupation. But by and large the Area's charm is unimpaired, its acceptance of modern living unquestioned. The villages really do look much the same as they did before World

War II, while the fields, woods and beaches have regained all their old beauty. The happy sounds of birds and insects in the heat of the summer seem to speak of many past decades when nature might be said to have owned the countryside. Now there are handsome peacocks living in the grounds of a remote house, and in its big old ornamental pond there are waterfowl as well as fish. Bathers can be seen in the summer in the blue sea which was the centre of so much turbulence, though the strong undertow caused by the ridged beaches prevents them from taking too many liberties; an occasional water-skier is to be seen and, although Slapton is not a yachting base, small sailing boats are sometimes there as well as fishing boats. Much further off shore, crossing over Start Bay, bigger ships are frequently in evidence. The farmlands of the South Hams are now as fruitful and prolific as ever they were for the climate in this part of Devon is kindly. It would be difficult today to pick out any part of the Area still showing signs of neglect and destruction.

Today, few of those who were concerned in the Evacuation can speak of it with much clarity. So many of them have gone, and those who remain have either forgotten or have 'put their memories behind them' as one man said. But this was war as the civilian saw it and although many other parts of the country suffered appalling destruction and mutilation, this disturbance of the South Hams was unique in its way. In this purely agricultural part an entire neighbourhood was emptied and, at very short notice, its occupants had to leave their homes and fields to neglect and to the hazards of war. Their story will go down in history.

The last word shall be given to a very old lady who said she had lived through three wars—'the Boer War, the one that followed on and this one.' Then, in the understatement of all time, she continued,

'And this one was a proper caper and no mistake!'

POSTSCRIPT
The Normandy Beaches

ELEVEN YEARS AFTER THE D DAY LANDINGS ON THE COAST of Normandy, empty cartridge cases and other pieces of metal were still occasionally being turned up on the sandy beaches there. Yet a visit paid at that time to this lovely stretch of coast showed how much parts of it resemble the shingle ridges of Slapton Sands in many respects. The hills rise gently behind, and the district seems to possess much of the peace which characterises that part of the Devon coastline upon which the mock battles were fought in 1944. But during the visit the wind got up, a storm arose and conditions were so much like those which must have prevailed on invasion day that it was only too easy to imagine the roar of guns, the cross-fire of bullets and shells, and the ghosts of soldiers tumbling out of the landing craft and swarming up the beaches. At one beach a little of Mulberry 'B' harbour still remained just off shore and seemed almost like a backcloth to these D Day battles.

In a country lane just above one of the beaches, again so like its Devon counterpart, was a large wooden building which had been erected as a museum. There were big photographs all round the walls—scenes of battle, of the ships lying just off the shore, of large groups of men running, or close-ups of individuals—giving a graphic description of the terrible fighting which took place there as on all the strategically selected beaches along the coast of the Cotentin Peninsula. There were pathetic photographs too, of exhausted and wounded men who had fallen in the battle.

The museum contained the flotsam and jetsam of any battlefield—a 'tin' hat, rifles and other firearms, together with many items which were left behind as the armies moved forward. The photos also showed some of the clearing up process necessary on the beaches as the fighting progressed inland, including the work of certain beach groups such as the RAMC and others responsible for the wounded in embarking as many as possible of these back to England, some of them having been struck down as soon as they had landed. Later there were many enemy prisoners of war to be sent to camps in the same way, and as the ships returned again to the peninsula they brought the many stores and different types of equipment necessary to back up the Allied advance. Petrol was conveyed in special ships, though as soon as the invasion had taken place successfully an underseas pipeline, known as Operation Pluto, was established from England to Normandy.

One of the most interesting items in the museum was a diorama in a long glass-topped case, running down the centre and length of the room. It was in the form of a contour map of the coasts of England and Northern France with the English Channel in between. When a group of people had gathered round this exhibit a curator plunged the room into complete darkness, and then little electric lights appeared on the English south coast where the Allied armies were assembled and waiting for embarkation orders. At the same time the sound was switched on and a man's voice, in French, described exactly what was happening. The lights came and went in tiny spurts and trails, representing the movements across the Channel—aeroplanes, ships, and thousands of troops landing all along the Cotentin peninsula. The great American success over the enemy at Cherbourg was described and then the arrival of the shiploads of stores essential for the replenishment of the troops.

In another room a film showing the story of the invasion was shown. This, the work of official, government-sponsored cameramen, will be a graphic piece of history for succeeding generations. It may serve as a warning perhaps against a future, even more terrible war.